FREEDOM TO REJOICE
UNDERSTANDING
ST JOHN OF THE CROSS

D1102177

NORBERT CUMMINS OCD

FREEDOM TO REJOICE

UNDERSTANDING
ST JOHN OF THE CROSS

Norbent Cummins OCD

HarperCollins*Religious*
An imprint of HarperCollins*Publishers*

First published in Great Britain in 1991
by HarperCollinsReligious
part of HarperCollinsPublishers
77–85 Fulham Palace Road, London W6 8JB

Copyright © 1991 Norbert Cummins OCD

The Author asserts the moral right
to be identified as the author of this work

Printed and bound in Great Britain
by HarperCollins Manufacturing, Glasgow

Conditions of Sale
This book is sold subject to the condition
that it shall not, by way of trade or otherwise,
be lent, re-sold, hired out or otherwise circulated
without the publisher's prior consent in any form of
binding or cover other than that in which it is
published and without a similar condition
including this condition being imposed
on the subsequent publisher.

CONTENTS

St John of the Cross did not write his works with a view to the investigation of scholars or those engaged in higher studies; they were written for the purpose of directing contemplatives toward union with God.

Karol Wojtyla,
Faith according to St John of the Cross
Ignatius Press,
San Francisco, 1981

PREFACE

A few years ago Darlington Carmel edited and published my booklet, *An Introduction to St John of the Cross*. It was intended for an audience that was more or less familiar with the tradition of Carmelite spirituality. Shortly after its publication I was asked to bring out a revised and enlarged edition for a wider public. The request for this came first from Dr Lucy O'Sullivan (Kensington) who offered some helpful suggestions for a rearrangement of the material and a more natural sequence of ideas. My hesitation to do the work was removed by encouragement from some of my Carmelite brethren, in view of the fourth centenary of St John of the Cross (died 1591). So I faced the task of revision, relying on the prayers of not a few Carmelite nuns.

Unexpected help turned up in the person of Dr Liz Carmichael, who spontaneously offered to assist in relating the work to its new audience. In spite of her scholarly commitment at Worcester College, Oxford, she found time to read through the revised chapters as they were completed. In addition, she did some laborious research on references and on a few doctrinal problems that arose in connection with the text. Her help and encouragement was invaluable. I gratefully acknowledge her contribution to the final product. I am grateful also to her friend, Jeremy Marshall, who sacrificed some of his precious time to read through several passages of doubtful clarity.

The revision of the original text has been considerable, and five new chapters have been added. After a preliminary chapter on reading St John of the Cross, there are three chapters introducing the basic themes of his teaching. These chapters should familiarize the reader with St John's terminology, before taking a look at his formal teaching in the chapters that follow. Some repetition was therefore inevitable but tolerable, I hope, in this kind of subject.

Carmelite Retreat Centre   Norbert Cummins OCD
Termonbacca, Derry, Northern Ireland
14 December 1990

ABBREVIATIONS

The Ascent of Mount Carmel   A.
The Dark Night   D.N.
The Spiritual Canticle   Sp.Cant.
The Living Flame of Love   L.F.

The text of St John of the Cross used throughout the book is
taken from:

The Collected Works of St John of the Cross, translated by Kieran
Kavanaugh and Otilio Rodriguez © 1979 by Washington
Province of Discalced Carmelites, ICS Publications, 2131
Lincoln Road, N.E. Washington D.C. 20002 U.S.A., cited as *K*.

BIOGRAPHICAL
INTRODUCTION

St John of the Cross was born in Spain in 1542, in the small town of Fontiveros, north-west of Avila. His father, Gonzalo de Yepes, came from a family of wealthy silk merchants, but his relatives disowned him when he married Catalina Alvarez, a weaver who had been left destitute on her parents' early death. The couple considered their love ample compensation for their poverty. Three sons were born, of whom two, Francis and his youngest brother John, survived their early years. Luis, the second son, died. After about ten years of devoted married life Gonzalo contracted an illness that lasted two years and drained the family's meagre resources. When he died Catalina found it difficult to earn enough for the support of her two sons, and when John had reached the age of nine she placed him in the Catechism School, a kind of orphanage, at Medina. He remained there for eight years, learning to read and write and trying his hand in turn as carpenter, tailor, wood-carver, and painter. In addition, he was obliged to beg on the streets for the upkeep of the school. When he was seventeen he took up nursing at one of Medina's hospitals. This involved first-hand contact with suffering, as well as collecting alms for the poor patients. He was able to study by attending the nearby Jesuit college for a few hours each day, and by reading late at night. That he was not embittered by the hardships of his lot is clear from the fact that when he was offered an easier career as chaplain to the hospital, he opted instead for membership of the Carmelite Order. After his novitiate he was sent to study at the University of Salamanca, and was ordained priest in 1567. He still wanted a more wholly contemplative life, and had his mind set on becoming a Carthusian.

It was at this moment, when he was twenty-five, that he met St Teresa. She persuaded him to become a founder member of the Discalced Carmelite Reform. For the next ten years he worked with her, beginning his life's work of teaching and spiritual formation of nuns, friars, and lay people. Although ecclesiastical permission had been granted for the Reform, it seemed like treason to some of the other Carmelite brethren. The authority of the Order's General Chapter of Piacenza was invoked against it, and St John was kidnapped on the night of 3 December 1577. He was taken as a prisoner to Toledo, where everything possible was done to make him renounce the Reform. His imprisonment lasted for nine months in an airless cell, with only a small opening high up for light. He suffered intensely at this time both physically and spiritually. The prison illustrated what was happening in his soul, and he used its imagery afterwards to describe the night of the spirit. Towards the end of his imprisonment, his jailer gave him a few scraps of paper on which he wrote down some verses he had composed at that time. From these we can guess the height of his spiritual attainment as he made the gift of himself to God.

> There He gave me His breast,
> There He taught me a sweet and living knowledge.
> And I gave myself to Him,
> Keeping nothing back;
> There I promised to be His bride.[1]

In his commentary on this stanza, St John later explained that the sweet and living knowledge Christ had taught him was "mystical theology, that secret knowledge of God which spiritual persons call contemplation". All of his written work dates from after this time. So it is primarily as a mystic in love with Christ that he is to be read and interpreted.

Unfortunately, the first edition of his published work (1618) was entitled *The Dark Night of the Soul*, with the result that St John came to be regarded as a teacher of negative spirituality, writing from his prison experience. In fact, the poem *One Dark Night* was not composed in the Toledo prison but some years later, amid the beauties of nature. There is nothing negative about it. It sings of the happiness of one who has departed from selfishness, "attracted by God and enkindled with love for Him alone".[2] It sings of "love's urgent longings", explaining "how easy, sweet, and delightful these longings for their Spouse make all the trials and dangers of the night seem".[3] St John's poetic genius surfaced first in his prison days. Among the compositions of that time were thirty-one stanzas of the *Spiritual Canticle*, inspired by a certain burning love of God, a love flowing from abundant mystical understanding.[4] These stanzas were fashioned as a result of the purifying fire of affliction and isolation, in the absence of any comfort from heaven or earth. They were the poetic outpouring of a human spirit that had been "humbled, softened and purified, until it became so delicate, simple, and refined that it could be one with the Spirit of God".[5] Only that kind of person could sing that kind of spiritual canticle. No other could perceive the tender love by which the heavenly Father exalts the loving soul. "No mother's affection, in which she tenderly caresses her child, nor brother's love, nor friendship is comparable to it."[6]

St John was not a professional writer. His major prose works were written with pastoral intent, at times when he was burdened with various responsibilities in the new Teresian Reform, as Rector of Baeza, Prior of Granada, and Vicar-Provincial of

Andalusia. He had to supervise new foundations of Carmelite houses and he was often seen helping the workmen on the building sites. Much of his time was taken up with spiritual direction and the work of his ministry as a Carmelite priest. Although there was an abundance of religious literature in sixteenth-century Spain, there was great misunderstanding on the essential requirement for union with God. The *Ascent of Mount Carmel* and the *Dark Night* were St John's remedy for this situation. "Some people – and it is sad to see them – work and tire themselves greatly, and yet go backwards; for they look for perfection in exercises that are of no profit to them, but rather a hindrance . . . because they do not willingly adapt themselves to God's work in placing them on the pure and reliable road leading to union."[7]

St John's essential textbook was the cross of Christ, in which he read the clearest revelation of God's infinite love. And so, when Christ appeared to him from the cross in Segovia and asked him what reward he wanted for some service rendered, he replied, "Lord, what I wish you to give me are sufferings to be borne for your sake, and that I may be despised and regarded as worthless". His prayer was heard. From that time onwards he was drawn into the redemptive sufferings of Christ. Calumnies were spread to discredit him, and there were rumours that he might be expelled from the Order. After the Madrid Chapter, he was sent more or less in disgrace to the solitude of La Penuela. In September he fell seriously ill and he chose the monastery of Ubeda for treatment, where he knew he would not encounter any special kindness.

During his last illness, his infirmarian sent for some musicians to alleviate the patient's sufferings, for it was well known that he loved music. The companions of his early journeys had recounted how he would often improvise songs to express the melodies in his heart. Now, however, the time for earthly music was past.

When the musicians arrived he said, "Thank them, and give them a meal". His mind was filled with another kind of music, and he knew that by the hour of Matins he would sing a new song in the life of glory.[8] He died on 14 December 1591.

NOTES

1   *Sp.Cant.*, stanza 27, *K.*, p. 518
2   I *A.*, 1/4, *K.*, p. 74
3   I *A.*, 14/3, *K.*, p. 105
4   *Sp.Cant.*, Prol. 1, 2, *K.*, pp. 408–9
    The following poems belong to St John's time in the Toledo prison: *For I Know Well the Spring*; nine *Romances*; and *On the Psalm, "By the Waters of Babylon"*. It is generally held that thirty-one stanzas of the *Spiritual Canticle* were composed at intervals during the same time. But see *St John of the Cross: His Life and Poetry* by Gerald Brenan, Cambridge University Press, 1973, pp. 101–2
5   II *D.N.*, 7/3, *K.*, p. 342
6   *Sp.Cant.*, 27/1, *K.*, p. 517
7   *Ascent*, Prol. 7, 3, *K.*, pp. 72, 70
8   *Sp.Cant.*, 39/10, *K.*, p. 560

1

READING ST JOHN
OF THE CROSS*

Those who read St John of the Cross for the first time can be put off by his writing. As a boy, he was apprenticed to various skills. Journalism was not one of them. When he wanted to express the love enkindled within him from the abundance of his mystical understanding, he poured out "secrets and mysteries" in a poetic medium that might be the envy of the greatest. But he did admit that his prose explanations were in a rough style, though that was not the chief cause of their obscurity. The beginner would find him difficult at first reading, he said, but "if he reads this work a second time the matter will seem clearer and the doctrine sounder". He knew that his doctrine was "good and very necessary" but that, even if he had written more elegantly, few would profit by it "because we are not writing on pleasing and delightful themes addressed to the kind of spiritual people who like to approach God along sweet and satisfying paths".[1]

It is not surprising that we hesitate to follow St John of the Cross into the totally unselfish realm of Christ's love. We feel uneasy with the words of our Lord himself when we reflect on the cost of discipleship. But what at first seems to be a heartless demand turns out to be the language of a most tender love, and it is our failure to grasp this love more than our fear of hardship that makes St John unpalatable reading. The half-hearted beginner will take offence at his severity. There is a sense in which St John of the Cross had no heart for himself: "He who is in love is said to have his heart stolen or seized by the object of his love, for his heart will go out of self and become fixed on the loved object. Thus his heart or love is not for himself, but for what he loves".[2] Whenever St John speaks "heartlessly" he is concerned with some disorder in relation to our union with God. While he is thinking of what we stand to gain, we have in mind perhaps what kind of sacrifice is demanded of us. Because we are not yet free, we read him apprehensively. His tastes had already been transformed in God before he began to write, and so he could not share our longing for earthly things. Instead, he multiplies arguments to convince us, knowing that our disordered appetites themselves hinder us from reasoning clearly about them. The truth of the situation is not left in doubt. Perfect union with God together with disordered attachment to creatures is an impossibility.

> A person is indeed ignorant if he thinks it is possible to reach this high state of union with God without first emptying his appetite of all natural and supernatural things which can be a hindrance to him . . . for the doctrine the Son of Man came to teach is contempt of all things, that we may receive the gift of God's Spirit.[3]

We must not mistake the rigour of St John's logic for a psychological rigorism. He was well aware that imperfect love is required to give only what it can. God does not demand the impossible. The total correction of all the appetites is not attained until a soul reaches perfect union with God. What grieved St John most was the thought that those who had received the grace to become detached from so much should afterwards fail in some smaller things which God wanted them to overcome for love of him, since these trifling things can in fact impede so great a good. "Oh, if people knew how much spiritual good and abundance they lose by not attempting to raise their appetite above childish things, and if they knew to what extent, by not desiring the taste of these trifles, they would discover in this simple spiritual food the savor of them all."[4] The totality of the sacrifice which he demands is simply the logic of the total end to which he would lead us.

Some readers think that St John of the Cross speaks too much about suffering. But our lack of fortitude is not his chief concern. He is thinking mostly of people who *are* suffering, and perhaps to no good purpose. There are right ways and wrong ways of being an ascetic, and he would save us a futile labour. "Some people – and it is sad to see them – work and tire themselves greatly, and yet go backwards; they look for perfection in exercises that are of no profit to them, but rather a hindrance."[5] Even the con-solations and favours of God given for advancing in perfection can become a hindrance. The joys and sorrows, the hopes and afflictions that are experienced on the spiritual road may be interpreted for good or ill. On all these issues St John pours light, combining delicacy with firmness. He speaks with the con-fidence of a master. We never get the impression that he is feeling his way, or that we shall have to revise our opinion later on. In fact, his statements are so definitive that they are sometimes taken for harshness. Like the prophets of old, he had first incarnated in himself the doctrine he was destined to impart, and his mature spiritual attainment influenced his style of writing.

For beginners and even for the proficient he writes objectively in a scientific idiom. When he treats of the perfect, his language becomes much less restricted until, introducing the *Living Flame*, it has become quite subjective: "Knowing the reader under-stands that everything I say is as far from the reality as is a painting from the living object represented, I shall venture to declare what I know".[6] He is never so objective or detached as to forget his reader. He frequently gives us hints how we should read him. These hints occur during the course of his teaching, sometimes when he reminds us for whom he is writing; sometimes when he qualifies a word to let us know its true meaning in the context. Particularly in the Prologues we find a useful key to what follows. Thus in the Prologue to the *Ascent*, admitting the obscurity of his doctrine at that stage, he gives advice: "This, I believe, will be the case as he begins to read, but as he reads on he will understand it better, since the latter parts will explain the former."[7] This means that we must keep in mind the general plan or movement of his thought, since the force of his argument depends, as in all moral matters, on the goal of the journey, "the latter parts explaining the former".

Accordingly, we may think of four keys for reading St John of the Cross: the general plan of his work, the kind of reader he had in mind, the reason why he wrote and, not least important, his idiom or mode of writing.

THE GENERAL PLAN

St John's writings fall naturally into two parts. The first part is the path leading to union with God, comprising the *Ascent of Mount Carmel* (three books) and the *Dark Night* (two books). The second is the experience of this union which he expressed in two poems, the *Spiritual Canticle* and the *Living Flame of Love*, with their commentaries. This second part may be described as a shared experience of the high state of union with God. Both parts are journeys of the soul, each with its own dynamism. The first is simply the departure from selfishness. The second is the dynamism of love itself, when the purified soul moves on towards the perfection of love in spiritual espousals and continues until it reaches spiritual marriage, the ultimate state of perfection.

Joining the two sections is the concept of union with God. An elaboration of this concept is not located at the end of the *Ascent-Night*, as one might expect, but in chapter five of II *Ascent*, where St John inserted it as a parenthesis in his treatment of the virtue of faith, because his argument could not proceed until the nature of divine union had been clarified. The first thing the reader has to do, then, is to take hold of this concept, noticing that St John has in mind the union and transformation of the soul in God. This takes place when God's will and the soul's are in conformity, so that nothing in the one is repugnant to the other and the soul, completely rid of selfishness, rests transformed in God through love.

Immediately after chapter five it would be useful to go on to chapter seven which shows that the extent of our self-denial corresponds to the intensity of union. It also shows that during the soul's journey, Christ himself is the teacher and the model, as well as the crown and reward at the end. St John is not putting forward any pet theory of his own, but the pure doctrine of the Gospel. He takes no pleasure in stressing the hardships of the way. He strives rather to make attractive and practical what he knows is solid and substantial teaching.

> O, who can make this counsel of our Saviour understandable, and practicable, and attractive that spiritual persons might become aware of the difference between the method many of them think is good and that which ought to be used in travelling this road . . . They think a denial of self in worldly matters is sufficient without an annihilation and purification of spiritual possessions.[8]

This is the mystery of the gate and the way that leads to union with God. For it was when Christ was most annihilated in all things that he accomplished the most marvellous work of his whole life, the reconciliation and union of the human race with God. "The journey, then, does not consist in recreations, experiences, and spiritual feelings, but in the living, sensory and spiritual, exterior and interior death of the cross."[9]

Just as Christ's death was for the sake of life, so the mystery of the gate and the way is a paschal mystery, whereby we pass over from a condition of slavery to the liberty of the children of God. St John's poem of the *Night* is the song of this deliverance. The metaphor of slavery used so effectively by St Paul in Romans and Galatians is a good key to the general plan of *Ascent-Night*. It preserves the excitement of the soul's journey and is included in St John's metaphor of the paschal night. St John frequently refers to our "wretched state of captivity" because of original sin. He calls it a "sheer grace" to be released from this prison without hindrance from the jailers. For a person attached to creatures "is considered and treated by God as a base slave and prisoner, not as a son. And freedom cannot abide in a heart dominated by the appetites – a slave's heart; it dwells in a liberated heart, which is a son's heart".[10]

The happiness of escape is the culmination of the two books of the *Dark Night*. St John considered his poem of the *Night* as a "summary of the doctrine expounded, a basis for all I shall say". It is the soul's song of joy celebrating its escape from the prison of self-love. It praises the night of its exodus in language comparable to the famous *Exultet* of Easter: "The power of this holy night dispels all evil, washes guilt away, restores lost innocence, it casts out hatred, brings us peace, and humbles earthly pride. Night truly blessed when heaven is wedded to earth and man is reconciled with God."[11] In St John's poem the night is celebrated because it was the guide on the way and the cause of union at the end:

> . . . night that joined the lover
> To the beloved bride
> Transfiguring them each into the other . . .[12]

11

THE READER ST JOHN HAD IN MIND

There has been some difference of opinion as to the kind of reader St John had in mind. In the Prologue to the *Ascent* he says that his "main intention is not to address everyone, but only some of the persons of our holy Order of the Primitive Observance of Mount Carmel, both friars and nuns, . . . since they are the ones who asked me to write this work".[13] Even if we see this only as his main intention, it seems to restrict his literary audience. A further restriction is implied in the words "some of the persons of our Holy Order", where the reason given is not that they belong to "our holy Order" but that "they are already detached to a great extent from the temporal things of this world and will more easily grasp this doctrine on the nakedness of spirit". This does not mean that they were contemplatives already, but they were at least beginners, and a beginner for St John of the Cross is the soul that God nurtures and caresses like a loving mother, "after it has been resolutely converted to His service".[14] He qualifies the state of beginners as those who practice meditation on the spiritual road. He goes to some trouble to describe the characteristics of beginners in order to help them understand the feebleness of their state and take courage and desire that God place them in the night where they may be strengthened. But when we read his well-known account of the imperfections of beginners, we recognize these as very fervent beginners, *after* they have been resolutely converted to God's service.

Like all spiritual writers, St John would have liked to help everyone on the way to God. His doctrine of the way to union with God has a universal character. "Our goal will be, with God's help, to explain all these points so that everyone who reads this book will in some way discover the road he is walking along." To this he adds a significant limitation: "and the one he ought to follow *if he wants to reach the summit of the mount*".[15] So everything said is not prescribed indiscriminately for everyone as a practical norm. Introducing the *Ascent-Night*, he proposes doctrine for both beginners and proficient. When laying down conditions for the emptiness of the faculties, he alerts the reader to the distinction between the two categories so that beginners may not imprudently attempt this exercise before their time.

> Remember that I am now addressing those especially who have begun to enter the state of contemplation ... Let us address the intellect of the spiritual man, particularly of him whom God has favoured with the state of contemplation, for, as I asserted, I am now speaking especially to these individuals.[16]

Much difficulty and misunderstanding could be avoided if we kept these warnings in mind. He repeats them frequently, for he is sensitive to the different times and phases on the spiritual journey. "In each of these books the reader must keep in mind the intention we have in writing. Failure to do so will give rise to many doubts about what he reads."[17] This has particular importance when putting his doctrine into practice. If a particular passage does not apply to our stage of the spiritual life, there are other good motives for reading St John's writings. The whole journey to God is of interest at any point on the way, since it is the story of a supreme love, terminating ultimately in perfect union with the Beloved. Even the most elementary beginner will appreciate the excitement of the adventure in divine love and marvel at its consummation.

WHY HE WROTE

In the Prologue to the *Ascent*, St John tells us that he is undertaking this arduous task "not because of any particular confidence in my own abilities. Rather, I am confident that the Lord will help me to explain this matter, because it is extremely necessary to so many souls".[18]

At the time he was writing there were many books on the practice of meditation and there were good accounts of perfect contemplation, but there was nothing worthwhile on the intervening stages. Particularly, there was great misunderstanding of the two transition periods or crises of growth, one of which marked the beginning of infused contemplation (*Night of Sense*) and the other which introduced the soul to perfect union with God (*Night of Spirit*). To St John's way of thinking, this situation was lamentable because of the amount of unprofitable suffering entailed and the failure of many to reach the perfection that God had destined for them. As he saw it, whole periods or parts of the journey, because of their obscurity and pain, were written off as mere psychological aberrations, or hangovers from a former life, or even as symptoms of God's displeasure. Because St John had pity for souls in this predicament, he felt obliged to offer help in writing. His discernment of God's ways and his zeal for the perfection of God's work in souls urged him to speak harshly of incompetent spiritual directors:

It will happen that while an individual is being conducted by God along a sublime path of dark contemplation and aridity, in which he feels lost, he will encounter in the midst of the fulness of his darknesses, trials, conflicts, and temptations, someone who, in the style of Job's comforters, will proclaim that all of this is due to melancholia, or depression, or temperament, or some hidden wickedness, and that as a result God has forsaken him. The director does not understand that now perhaps is not the time for such activity. Indeed, it is a period for leaving these persons alone in the purgation God is working in them, a time to give comfort and encouragement that they may desire to endure this suffering as long as God wills, for until then, no remedy – whatever the soul does, or the confessor says – is adequate.[19]

It comes as a surprise to discover that, in his commentary on the *Living Flame*, of all places, St John "indulged" in a lengthy digression on the harm done by incompetent directors. It is only at an exalted level that the gravity of the situation can be rightly assessed, "a damage beyond anything imaginable". The harm done is greater and worthy of deeper sorrow than the disturbance and ruin of many ordinary souls. Because of the refined nature of God's sublime working in the soul at this time, neither the soul itself nor its spiritual director understands it. What prompted St John to write these pages on spiritual direction was his knowledge of the mysterious, delicate working of the Holy Spirit in human souls. Any damage done in this area is "all seriously harmful and a great sorrow and pity".[20]

HIS IDIOM OR MODE OF WRITING

The terms used in mystical theology were already more or less established by the time St John began to write. Mystical writers, having no words for ineffable realities, had taken over the terms of philosophy and theology but gave them a significance proper to their own realm of mysticism. Being a science of experience, its language represented the psychological registration of the mystics rather than abstract concepts. Thus the "sensory" and the "spiritual" are realms of experience rather than philosophical categories. The mystic recognizes "parts" of the soul which, for the philosopher, is a simple, indivisible substance. A certain depth of mystical experience will open a new realm of consciousness which the mystic will refer to as the "substance" of the soul. To confuse this with the philosopher's notion of substance would be mistaken idiom. A similar confusion follows if we interpret St John's use of the word "infused" as belonging to the idiom of dogmatic theology. For example, "infused contemplation" is not a reference to the supernatural principle of infused virtue, nor to the supernatural object of virtue, but to the supernatural mode, that is, to "how" the contemplative has come by this experience. The mysterious "how" of infused contemplation is beyond ordinary explanation, and the word "infused" has to be used as the nearest psychological approximation.

It is also worth noting that St John's abundant use of figures and similes in his later commentaries was purposely designed to leave his "explanation" open, so that each one could derive profit from it.

> Though we give some explanation of these stanzas, there is no need to be bound to this explanation. For mystical wisdom, which comes through love ... need not be understood distinctly in order to cause love and affection in the soul, for it is given according to the mode of faith through which we love God without understanding Him.[21]

Since mystical wisdom is given according to the mode of faith and love, which is beyond human understanding, the language of the mystics never adequately expresses what they want to say. The most they can do is to "let something of their experience overflow in figures and similes". From this we may deduce a final key for reading the writings of St John of the Cross: whenever he expresses his meaning in figures and similes, these must be read with the simplicity of the spirit of knowledge and love they contain.[22]

---

* Author's Note: This chapter was first written for *Mount Carmel* magazine (Autumn 1980) and is reproduced here with permission of the Editor.

NOTES

1   *Ascent* Prol. 8, *K.*, p. 72
2   *Sp.Cant.*, 9/5, *K.*, p. 444
3   I *A.*, 5/2, *K.*, p. 81
4   I *A.*, 5/4, *K.*, p. 82
5   I *A.*, Prol. 7, *K.*, p. 72
6   *L.F.* Prol. 1, *K.*, p. 577
7   I *A.*, Prol. 8, *K.*, p. 72
8   II *A.*, 7/5, *K.*, p. 122
9   II *A.*, 7/11, *K.*, p. 125
10 I *A.*, 4/6, *K.*, p. 80
11 See article *Night and Light: the poet John of the Cross and the Exultet of Easter*, by John Sullivan in *Ephemer. Carm.* XXX 52
12 Roy Campbell translation
13 I *A.*, Prol. 9, *K.*, p. 72
14 I *D.N.*, 1/2, *K.*, p. 298
15 I *A.*, Prol. 7, *K.*, p. 72
16 II *A.*, 6/8, *K.*, p. 121; II *A.*, 7/13, *K.*, p. 125
17 III *A.*, 2/1, *K.*, p. 214
18 I *A.*, Prol. 3, *K.*, p. 70
19 I *A.*, Prol. 4, 5, *K.*, p. 71
20 *L.F.*, 3/41, *K.*, p. 625
21 *Sp.Cant.*, Prol. 2, *K.*, p. 409
22 *Sp.Cant.*, Prol. 1, *K.*, p. 408

2

UNION WITH GOD

The beginning is revealed from the viewpoint of the end;
ultimately, it is revealed only thus; the beginning is the
beginning of the end.[1]

Karl Rahner

The first great religious truth we learn is that we were made for
God. Our call into existence was our call to union with God. For
St John of the Cross, this end or purpose of our being is a union
of love. We were created for love.[2] Because St John took this to
be the end of our life's journey, the major part of his writings
consists of commentaries on three love-poems, the *Dark Night*,
the *Spiritual Canticle*, and the *Living Flame*. His minor works
include *Sayings of Light and Love, Maxims on Love*, and *Romances*
on God's love story in creation and redemption.

Some passages in his writings seem to recommend a way that
is rigorous and forbidding, but he merely states facts that are
certain. "The soul must ordinarily walk this path to reach that
sublime and joyous union with God."[3] His doctrine of the way
seems at first sight to restrict our freedom. But when we examine
the *Ascent of Mount Carmel* and the *Dark Night of the Soul*, we find
that they are concerned almost entirely with liberation, so that
the soul can go out from self in search of the living God, and
ultimately embrace him in a union of love. The aim of St John's
rigour is true human freedom, the freedom to love; not only to
love God but also to love and enjoy the world that he made, in the
way it should be loved and enjoyed.[4] In the *Spiritual Canticle* and

the *Living Flame*, St John describes his own experience of that freedom, and the theological dynamics of his love-search for God. For him, the way to true freedom is a paschal mystery on the model of Christ's death and resurrection. The *Dark Night* poem is like an Easter *Exultet*, or like the Canticle of Moses after the liberation of his people. "The soul, through original sin, is a captive in the mortal body, subject to passions and natural appetites; when liberated from this bondage and submission, it considers its escape . . . a sheer grace."[5] It is the grace of a new freedom for the ascent of the soul to God, for these passions "afflict the soul with their chains, and they will prevent it from soaring to the liberty and repose of sweet contemplation and union".[6]

The Exodus was only the beginning of the people's journey. It took on a new meaning when they approached Mount Sinai. "And the Lord came down upon Mount Sinai, to the top of the mountain; and the Lord called Moses to the top of the mountain, and Moses went up."[7] The ascent of the mountain, even more than the Exodus, became the favourite image of the spiritual life. By the time of St Gregory of Nyssa (died AD 394) it was already part of the tradition in Christian spirituality.

He who would approach the knowledge of things sublime must first purify his manner of life from all sensual and irrational emotion. He must wash from his understanding every opinion derived from some preconception and withdraw himself from his customary intercourse with his own companion, that is, with his sense perceptions, which are, as it were, wedded to our nature as its companion. When he is so purified, then he assaults the mountain.
The knowledge of God is a mountain steep indeed and difficult to climb – the majority of people scarcely reach its base.[8]

The *Ascent of Mount Carmel* by St John of the Cross has its place in this tradition. St John makes all the traditional demands. The beginner's first steps must be the cleansing of the mind and the withdrawal of the heart from irrational desire. We are left in no doubt about the exalted height of the mountain and the difficulty of the climb. The emphasis is upon release from inordinate attachments and desires instead of extraordinary penances. The purpose of this inner "mortification" is to set the soul free for God. St John lamented the ignorance of those who "burden themselves with extraordinary penances and many other exercises, thinking they are sufficient for the attainment of union with the divine wisdom . . . If these people would attempt to devote only a half of that energy to the renunciation of their desires, they would profit more in a month than in years with all these other exercises".[9]

In the first pages of the *Ascent*, St John tells the reader that the top of the mountain, the high state of perfection, will be called "union of a soul with God",[10] and the phrase keeps recurring right through his works. Just as a person making a journey to a certain city will search for the name of that city on every signpost, so St John keeps the end of the journey in mind at every turn. The experience of union is described in the *Spiritual Canticle* and the *Living Flame of Love*; the way to union in the *Ascent of Mount Carmel* and the *Dark Night*. The *Ascent* and the *Night* are mainly in the form of argument, and the conclusions are always drawn from the end of the journey. The presumption is that the reader wants to reach the end but may lack the knowledge of how to go about it. For, in the time of St John of the Cross, ascetical practices were the accepted thing among religious people: one must be detached from the things of earth in order to gain the things of heaven. But it was not so clear that even heavenly things (spiritual goods and divine consolations) could also become obstacles. St John noticed that some were content with a certain degree of virtue, perseverance in prayer and mortification, but they continued to "feed and clothe their natural selves with spiritual feelings and consolations rather than divesting and denying themselves of these for God's sake".[11] The gifts of God are not God himself, and so the self-denial must be complete in both sense and spirit if a person wants to reach the summit of the mount.

St John uses slightly different expressions for the high state of union, but the differences are not significant. His meaning is clear. He does not mean pantheistic union, or any identification with God where the real distinction between the soul and God is blurred. Neither does he mean the natural union that always exists between the Creator and whatever he has created. In this sense, God is always united with everything created, holding it in being. Obviously excluded is the hypostatic union which is proper to Christ alone, and which is the source of our union with God. Even from the highest state of union in the present life St John excludes any transient phase of the beatific vision. The perfect soul is still a pilgrim of faith in this life. But even for the pilgrim soul there can be a tender and intimate friendship with God that is almost incredible, though the degree of intimacy varies in each case, "for not all souls attain an identical degree of union".[12]

How intimate this union can be is wonderfully illustrated in the pages of the *Spiritual Canticle* and the *Living Flame*. But it is clear also in the *Ascent* when St John speaks explicitly of union and uses the famous illustration of the window and the sun's rays. The glass in a window is a distinct entity, but when it is clean and polished we see through it as if it did not exist. The sun's light is so identified with the glass that they appear to be one and the same. The purified soul is like the polished glass. When God enlightens it, it will be transformed. "And God will so communicate His supernatural being to it that it will appear to be God Himself and will possess all that God Himself has . . . and the soul appears to be God more than a soul. Indeed, it is God by participation."[13] But when the soul is not cleansed from the smears and dust of inordinate desire for created things, God's light does not have the same effect upon it. From this, St John draws an important conclusion about the nature of love: "A man makes room for God by wiping away all the smudges and smears of creatures, by uniting his will perfectly to God's; for to love is to labour to divest and deprive oneself for God of all that is not God".[14]

Union with God is like the union of a loving husband and wife. What the one does is motivated by the wishes of the other. In the state of union with God, the soul is motivated "in all and through all" by the will of God. There is union of likeness in willing the same things. Thus the two wills are one. "And this one will is God's which becomes also the soul's. If a man should desire an imperfection unwanted by God, this one will of God would be destroyed because of the desire for what God does not will."[15] Just as love in married life does not consist so much in sweet exchanges of affection as in the self-denial of yielding to the other's wishes, so also in St John's doctrine, "to love is to labour to divest and deprive oneself for God of all that is not God". This is where many of the tragedies of life begin: the refusal to let go of some selfish attachment or desire. St John sees this tragedy in the case of some people called to close union with God.

> It is a matter for deep sorrow that, while God has bestowed on them the power to break other stronger cords of attachment to sins and vanities, they fail to attain so much good because they do not become detached from some childish thing which God has requested them to conquer for love of Him . . .[16]

> It makes little difference whether a bird is tied by a thin thread or by a cord. For even if tied by thread, the bird will be

prevented from taking off just as surely as if it were tied by cord . . . This is the lot of a man who is attached to something; no matter how much virtue he has he will not reach the freedom of the divine union.[17]

In St John's teaching, the chief benefit of detachment from creatures is "freedom of the heart for God".[18] The freedom must be complete if the union with God is to be perfect.

St John was saddened by the thought that some people, for such trivial reasons, obstructed the great work of God in their souls. Nevertheless, his writings are not focused on human failure. He had much experience of the brighter side of the story, which surfaces increasingly as his writings proceed. In fact, the enterprise of the spiritual climb is a success story for St John. No other spiritual writer has described so clearly the final stages of the ascent, and the happiness of the soul as it approaches the summit of the mountain of God. However, even at the summit of perfection in the present life, the soul is still a pilgrim of faith, and so its union with God cannot be absolutely perfect, "although it is beyond words and thought".[19]

NOTES

1 *Meditations on Hope and Love*, London, Burns and Oates, 1976, p. 35
2 See *Sp. Cant.*, 29/3, *K.*, p. 524
3 *D.N.*, Prologue, *K.*, p. 296
4 III *A.*, 20/2, *K.*, p. 247
5 I *A.*, 15/1, *K.*, p. 105
6 III *A.*, 16/6, *K.*, p. 239
7 Exodus 19/20
8 *Life of Moses*, 157, 158, Classics of Western Spirituality, p. 93
9 I *A.*, 8/4, *K.*, p. 90
10 I *A.*, Theme, *K.*, p. 68

11 II *A.*, 7/5, *K.*, p. 122
12 II *A.*, 5/10, *K.*, p. 118
13 II *A.*, 5/7, *K.*, p. 117
14 II *A.*, 5/7, *K.*, p. 117
15 I *A.*, 11/3, *K.*, p. 96
16 I *A.*, 11/5, *K.*, p. 97
17 I *A.*, 11/4, *K.*, p. 97
18 III *A.*, 20/4, *K.*, p. 248
19 *Sp.Cant.*, 22/4, *K.*, p. 497

3

CHRIST, THE WAY

> Since otherwise we should not find him, together with us he
> took our way to him. He did so to find a proper ending, for
> that end in Jesus also became our beginning.
>
> Karl Rahner[1]

Union of the soul with God, "the most noble and sublime state
attainable in this life",[2] is the goal of our spiritual journey. The
way to that goal is Jesus Christ. The end of the journey is also
union with the Word Incarnate. Jesus therefore is the focal point
of all of St John of the Cross's teaching. We are to establish our
wills "in humble love, and suffering in imitation of the life and
mortification of the Son of God. This is the road to the
attainment of every spiritual good".[3] Of our Lord's earthly life,
St John selects chiefly his sufferings and death, because they
spoke to him more clearly of Christ's love. The paschal mystery
of Christ's own journey to the Father has to be taken as the
model for every Christian. St John accordingly did not hesitate to
emphasize the cross, so that "the true spiritual person might
understand the mystery of the door and way (which is Christ)
leading to union with God".[4]

We need strong resolution to enter by the narrow gate; our
natural tendency is for the broad and easy way. We know
theoretically that the cross must be part of our Christian life, but
to accept it in practice is another matter. This will never be a
popular option. As Cardinal Newman said, it is more natural for
a civilized age to take the brighter side of the Gospel – its tidings

of comfort and its precepts of love – and to forget all the darker, deeper views of man's condition.[5] Because St John of the Cross keeps this deeper view in mind, many feel he is out of touch with our time. What he presents is no more and no less than the challenge of our Lord's own life and teaching.

It is sometimes claimed that, whereas St Teresa is closer to the Synoptics, St John prefers the Fourth Gospel and St Paul. Certainly St Teresa was more at home with the historical Christ. She liked to keep him company at Jacob's well or in the garden of Gethsemane. St John was more attracted to the total mystery of Christ, to what he found in St Paul, in the Letter to the Hebrews, and in our Lord's prayer of consecration (John 17). The historical figure of Christ is more prominent in the writings of St Teresa, but St John's theology of Christ is more profound. Yet the historical Christ was very dear also to St John. The earthly life of Jesus was the model and the justification for many of his "hard sayings", especially in the *Ascent-Night*. Later, in the *Spiritual Canticle* and the *Living Flame*, the profundity of the Christian mystery takes over, when John relates our union with God directly to the hypostatic union in Christ. "The rock mentioned here, as St Paul says, is Christ (1 Corinthians 10:4). The high caverns of this rock are the sublime, exalted, and deep mysteries of God's wisdom in Christ, in the hypostatic union of the human nature with the divine Word, and in the correspond-ing union of men with God."[6] To bring out the depth of this mystery, St John uses the image of an abundant mine. There is so much to fathom in Christ that however deep men go they never reach the end, but find new veins of new riches in all directions. However wonderful the discoveries of saints and theologians in this life there will always be much more to discover in Christ.[7] In the hierarchy of graces, the wisdom of God given to us in Christ is supreme. All other spiritual activity, or fortitude in suffering, or favours from God are no more than preparations for this wisdom. For this is to behold "the revelation of the glory of God in the face of Jesus Christ".[8]

When we say that St John's theology of Christ is profound, we do not mean abstract, or that his own relationship with Christ lacked intimacy or tenderness. His personal love for Christ grew out of his contemplation of the crucifix. Sometimes he could not resist expressing this love by carving crucifixes, several of them the result of mystical experience. "On one occasion when he was contemplating Christ's dolourous cross, the Crucified One appeared to him in a corporal vision, covered with wounds and blood ... When John recovered from his ecstasy, he made a sketch, with a sort of Indian ink, which is now venerated in the Convent of the Incarnation."[9] The foreshortening of the figure gives the effect of a crucifix held to the lips of a dying person; the Christ on St John's drawing is not upright and indifferent but leaning sympathetically over the illness of a dying world in order to overwhelm its ingratitude with a still greater love, and thus draw out love in return.

That the Saint himself experienced this tenderness of Christ's love is clear from many incidents in his life. One day, upon entering a certain convent, he saw hanging on the wall a symbolic picture of the Passion of Christ, according to the allegory of the prophet Isaiah (Isaiah 63). Christ, like a bunch of grapes, was pouring out his blood beneath the weight of the cross, which was depicted as the beam of a winepress. The picture made such an impression on John that he was overwhelmed by wonder and love. The same delicate symbol had been used by some of the Fathers of the Church; the Word of God was likened to a great cluster of grapes pressed out for us. The image brings to mind the kind of wine St John had tasted in the cross. The fragrance of it pervades his writings.

Love is the centre of the whole economy of salvation: that is what the crucifix meant for St John of the Cross. The Church and the Christian life are extensions of the mystery through time. The truths of faith by which we live are so many aspects of a dialogue of love between God the Father and the human race. In that dialogue, Christ is the final and definitive Word, spoken to us "in these last days". St John follows the Letter to the Hebrews in his remarkable statement of the definitive character of the Christian revelation:

> In giving us His Son, His only Word (for He possesses no other), He spoke everything to us at once in this sole Word – and He has no more to say.[10]

> Any person questioning God or desiring some vision or revelation would not only be guilty of foolish behaviour but also of offending Him, by not fixing his eyes entirely on Christ and by living with the desire for some other novelty. God could respond as follows: If I have already told you all things in My Word, My Son, and if I have no other word, what answer or revelation can I now make that would surpass this? Fasten your eyes on Him alone, because in Him I have spoken and revealed all, and in Him you shall discover even more than you ask for and desire ... For He is my entire locution and response, vision and revelation, which I have already spoken, answered, manifested, and revealed to you, by giving Him to you as a brother, companion, master, ransom, and reward.[11]

In an age when visions, revelations, and spiritual consolations were the touchstone of divine approval, St John appealed to the example of Christ's own life. It was at the moment of his extreme abandonment on the cross that Christ "accomplished the most marvellous work of His whole life, surpassing all the works and deeds and miracles that He had ever performed on earth or in heaven".[12] The lesson is obvious: the road that leads to God is not simply a road of delightful spiritual experiences, but self-denial in spiritual goods as well as in material things and sense pleasure. St John knew that this was not a very acceptable doctrine. "I will not enlarge upon this, though I would like to continue discussing the matter, because from my observations Christ is to a great extent unknown by those who consider themselves His friends. Because of their extreme self-love they go about seeking in Him their own consolations and satisfactions. But they do not seek, out of great love for Him, His bitter trials and deaths."[13]

The love that St John saw in the crucifix was more than an accepting, suffering love. It was the triumph of love itself over sin and hatred. Jesus "in his own body of flesh and blood has broken down the enmity which stood like a dividing wall"[14] not only between rival human factions but between us and God. For St John, the whole creation is lifted up in the lifting up of Christ, and through the glory of his resurrection is clothed anew in beauty and dignity. "Not only by looking at them did He communicate natural being and graces ... but also with this image of His Son alone, He clothed them in beauty by imparting to them supernatural being. This He did when He became man and elevated human nature in the beauty of God and consequently all creatures, since in human nature He was united to them all."[15] This dignity and beauty of creation can be perceived only by a mind that is not "blinded by the god of this passing age".[16] When the faith of the believing mind is purified, its vision of the created world is perfected so that it can see the glory of the Lord in the cross of Jesus Christ.

What does "the glory of the Lord" mean? For sure it is the cross on which Christ was glorified, Christ the brightness of the Father's glory, as he himself said when he came to his passion: "Now is the Son of man glorified, and in him God is glorified and God will glorify him at once", meaning here by "glory" his being lifted up on the cross. The glory of Christ is the cross and his being lifted up, for he says: "And I, when I am lifted up, will draw all men to myself".[17]

NOTES

1   *Meditations on Hope and Love*, London, Burns and Oates, 1976, p. 73
2   II *A.*, 7/11, *K.*, p. 125
3   II *A.*, 29/9, *K.*, p. 206
4   II *A.*, 7/11, *K.*, p. 125
5   "What is the world's religion now? It has taken the brighter side of the Gospel, – its tidings of comfort, its precepts of love; all the darker, deeper views of man's condition and prospects being comparatively forgotten. This is the religion natural to a civilized age, and well has Satan dressed and completed it into an idol of Truth." *Plain and Parochial Sermons*, X 311, 1832
6   *Sp.Cant.*, 37/3, *K.*, p. 550
7   *Sp.Cant.*, 37/4, *K.*, p. 551
8   2 Corinthians 4:6, NEB
9   Fr Bruno ODC *St John of the Cross*, Sheed and Ward, 1936, p. 133. This drawing is reproduced as the frontispiece to the Kavanaugh translation of St John's works, and it inspired Salvador Dali's painting "Christ of St John of the Cross"
10   II *A.*, 22/3, *K.*, p. 179
11   II *A.*, 22/5, *K.*, p. 180
12   II *A.*, 7/11, *K.*, p. 124
13   II *A.*, 7/12, *K.*, p. 125
14   Ephesians 2:14, NEB
15   *Sp.Cant.*, 5/4, *K.*, p. 435
16   2 Corinthians 4:4, NEB
17   St Andrew of Crete, Or 9, On the Psalms; in *The Divine Office* III, p. 770, (Readings, Tuesday 33)

4

THE DARK NIGHT

The silent night which would otherwise seem sinister and threatening becomes the quiet closeness of the infinite mystery of our existence, which is both sheltering love and inconceivable grandeur.

Karl Rahner[1]

"In the first place it should be known that if a person is seeking God, his Beloved is seeking him much more."[2] This basic statement of St John of the Cross explains his frequent reference to the dark night, for the dark night is the means used by God to seek the soul "much more" and bring it to divine union. In St John's writings, the word "night" has various meanings. God himself is a dark night to us in this present life. The road we travel, namely faith, is night for our intellect. The various privations we undergo in checking our inordinate desires or tendencies are also a kind of night.[3] The means we use to reach God, the privations involved in our search for him, affect both our sense life and our intellect. So we have an active work to do at the level of sense and at the level of spirit. God also does his part at both these levels, his work running concurrently with ours. Thus we speak of an active and passive night of sense, and of an active and passive night of spirit. The word "passive" in these cases does not mean that we lack a vital role, but that God is the principal agent and we respond as receivers.

SENSE AND SPIRIT

A person with various abilities is sometimes referred to as a person "of many parts". In the same way St John of the Cross speaks of a sensory part and a spiritual part of the soul, even though the soul is a single whole and not made up of parts.[4]

The distinction of "sense" and "spirit" in St John's terminology is not quite the same as in the scholastic philosophy on which he partly depends. In both, the word "sense" is used for the level on which we perceive and respond to material, bodily objects. On this level we use the five exterior senses, and the "interior senses" which for St John are the fantasy and the imagination.[5] These two are the powers of imaging and of discursive thought that are used in meditation; they are open to both sense and spirit but can only mediate supernatural realities in terms of images derived from sense experience. On the level of spirit it is possible for the human person to perceive and respond to supernatural reality in faith, hope, and love. St John follows the Augustinian tradition in speaking about this level in terms of the three spiritual faculties of intellect, memory and will.[6] But whereas for philosophy "spirit" means complete immateriality, that is, total independence of bodily conditions (quantity, time, and place), for St John and for spiritual writers in general it denotes only a relative independence, unless the words "pure spirit" or "purely spiritual" are used.

This relative independence can be illustrated by the growth of knowledge in the intellect. As a spiritual faculty, the intellect is essentially immaterial and independent of matter, and even in its ordinary activity of reasoning it is fundamentally intuitive. However, the human intellect depends on data from the bodily senses for the development of its intuitive power. It begins this development with a simple grasp of its object by means of a concept or idea; by comparing two of these "simple apprehensions" it forms a judgement; by comparing judgements it arrives at a conclusion and so moves forward to new knowledge. This new knowledge, now experienced as intuitive light in the understanding, can continue to be incremented in this way until dependence on the reasoning process diminishes and we are left with the intuitive light only, in contemplation of what has been discovered by reason.[7] This is the level of "spirit", on which prayer ceases to be meditative and begins to be a "loving, general knowledge or awareness of God".

ACTIVE NIGHTS

On the journey to union with God, a person must be purified and illumined in both sense and spirit. The prayer that corresponds to the active night of the senses is meditation, the prayer of beginners:

> A person in this state should be given matter for meditation and discursive reflection, and he should by himself make interior acts and profit in spiritual things from the delight and satisfaction of the senses. For by being fed with the relish of spiritual things, the appetite is torn away from sensual things and weakened in regard to the things of the world.[8]

When its work is completed the active night of sense culminates in the setting aside of discursive thought and images.[9] In the active night of spirit, the soul is no longer helped by the considerations of reason and has to rely on faith, hope, and love. Contemplation is the characteristic prayer of this time. "The considerations, meditations, and acts which formerly helped the soul now hinder it, and it brings to prayer no other support than faith, hope and love."[10]

Even though we experience the active night of sense as privation, the purpose of it is positive, to establish the primacy of reason in our life, to direct our love and make us more human. In I *Ascent*, St John's instructions for the correction of our disordered desires are designed to perfect reason, to remove ignorance, weakness and defilement; in other words, to increase our intuitive power in grasping what is essential on the spiritual journey. This is the realm of the four traditional moral virtues which place reason rather than emotion or instinct in control.[11] Temperance makes us reasonable or moderate in our life-style. Fortitude keeps us reasonable in times of crisis, when great deeds have to be done or great sufferings to be endured. Justice makes us reasonable in our dealings with others so that we respect their rights. Prudence indicates where the reasonable course of action lies and does not allow our emotional tendencies to divert us from it.

When the harmony of reason is thus established, we are confronted with another and more difficult task, the submission of our reason to God, that is, to God's loving plan for our life. God's thoughts are so different from ours that we need some kind of super-reason if we are to understand and accept his sovereignty in our lives. This is the realm of the theological virtues. Faith, hope and charity lift us above the purely ethical standard and make us participate in God's way of thinking. They are divine powers and so are proportionate to divine union. What St John calls the active night of spirit consists chiefly in the exercise of these virtues. They alone can take us beyond our own narrow, "reasonable" thoughts, so that we can embrace God's loving plan. This does not mean that reason is cast aside. The theological virtues perfect our nature and give it a new dignity. Even at the highest levels of supernatural endowment, the role of reason remains intact. It cannot be too often emphasized that the mystics are very down-to-earth people. The attempt to by-pass reason and acquire knowledge by supernatural means has been a characteristic defect of various heretical sects, and has been severely censured by St John of the Cross:

> There is no necessity for any of this kind of knowledge, since a person can get sufficient guidance from natural reason, and the law and doctrine of the Gospel. There is no difficulty or necessity unsolvable or irremediable by these means, which are very pleasing to God. We should make such use of reason and the law of the Gospel that, even though – whether we desire it or not – some supernatural truths are told to us, we accept only what is in harmony with reason and the Gospel law. And then we should receive this truth, not because it is privately revealed to us, but because it is reasonable, and we should brush aside all feeling pertinent to the revelation.[12]

PASSIVE NIGHTS

St John introduces the passive night of sense by showing that even the fervent beginner, working with the help of ordinary grace, may still be a long way from perfection. God must intervene, for the soul's imperfections are of such a kind that only God can cure them. The cure will be a dark night for the soul. When God begins to act, his total otherness, his holiness, will break down the beginner's preconceived notions of holiness. Desires for spiritual consolation, self-confidence because of virtue acquired, and other failures of a similar kind will have to be purified. It will seem to the soul that all its former lights have vanished. The new dimension of God's intervention will contradict many of the soul's good intentions. The dark night "signifies here purgative contemplation, which passively causes in the soul this negation of self and of all things".[13] This infused contemplation does a divine work in the soul, which could not be done by human effort. The mysterious, purifying activity of God is a free gift. It enfolds the soul darkly in divine light and love, transforming its human activity so that eventually it can be one with the activity of God in the state of divine union.

St John thinks of the night primarily as a means to divine union and he relates it directly to the mystery of God's love. He does not conceal the depths of suffering and affliction caused by the night, and he describes with sensitivity the dereliction of the soul. The passive night of the spirit, the dark night properly speaking, is the privilege of very few. St John is almost alone in mapping out this part of the journey. Those who have some experience of this night will understand his language, and find comfort in the thought that others have been this way before. It is one thing to know the height of a mountain from a map, but quite another to experience the terror and exaltation of the climb. St John's experience lends authority to his words. He can remove obstacles and stumbling blocks from the paths of many souls who unknowingly trip and unconsciously walk in the path of error. He describes the need for the dark night, its causes and effects, and how secure the soul is in the darkness. His words are discretion for the wayfarer, light for the way, love in the wayfaring.[14]

NOTES

1 *Meditations on Hope and Love*, Burns and Oates, 1976, p. 74

2 *L.F.*, 3/28, *K.*, p. 620

3 See I *A.*, 2/1, *K.*, p. 74

4 I *A.*, 1/2, *K.*, p. 73

5 II *A.*, 12/3, *K.*, p. 137. Sensible memory is mentioned in *Sp. Cant.*, 18/7, *K.*, p. 484

6 This traditional threefold division of the faculties of the soul into memory, intellect (understanding) and will (the power to desire and choose, and therefore the power to love), originates with St Augustine (*De Trinitate*, Book 10)

7 See Chapter 10 of II *Ascent* where St John lists the apprehensions and

ideas comprehensible to the intellect, from the level of sense to that of spirit

8 *L.F.*, 3/32, *K.*, p. 621

9 See II *A.*, Chapters 13 and 14, *K.*, pp. 140, 142; I *D.N.*, 9 and 10, *K.*, p. 313, 316

10 *Maxims on Love*, 40, *K.*, p. 676

11 These four moral virtues, first called "cardinal" virtues by St Ambrose (d. 397 AD), were taken into Christian ascetic teaching from Greek philosophy. St John could assume that beginners in the spiritual life in his time would be striving for them. His own writing concentrates on the three Christian virtues of faith, hope and love (1 Corinthians 13:13), which were first called "theological" virtues by a scholastic theologian, William of Auxerre, about 1215 AD

12 II *A.*, 21/4, *K.*, p. 174

13 I *D.N.*, Explanation 1, *K.*, p. 297

14 *Sayings of Light and Love*, Prologue, *K.*, p. 666

5

THE PRECAUTIONS

Thomas Merton was fond of reading St John of the Cross even before he entered the Abbey of Gethsemani. After five or six years of monastic life, he realized the merit of St John's *Precautions*, and wrote about them in his *Spiritual Journal*: "They seem to me to be the most detailed and concrete and practical set of rules for arriving at religious perfection that I have ever seen".[1]

The *Precautions* are a programme for contemplative religious life. With some personal adaptation they can be of help to any reader, because they are about some of the fundamental attitudes and perspectives that promote peaceful and constructive relationships with other people, one's self, and the world of things. They tend to create a contemplative atmosphere. According to the testimony of Mother Anne of Jesus, they were written for the Carmelite nuns of Beas while St John was confessor there. But the gender throughout is masculine and this has led to the opinion that they were written for the friars of El Calvario where St John was Prior. As with the diagram of the *Mount*, he may well have made similar copies for both friars and nuns.

They are practical instructions, not a theory. St John is giving guidance to a young religious who thinks he sees his way towards union with God and wants to reach his goal in a short time. The programme consists of precautions or warnings about certain areas where the beginner will need to open his eyes a bit wider if he wishes to attain in a short time holy recollection and spiritual silence, nakedness, and poverty, where one enjoys the peaceful comfort of the Holy Spirit, reaches union with God, is freed from all obstacles incurred from the creatures of this world, defended against the wiles and deceits of the devil, and liberated from oneself.[2]

The kind of beginner whom St John is addressing is already clear from the spiritual level of the language he is using – *holy recollection* and *spiritual silence, nakedness and poverty*. He presupposes one who has been called by God and desires to respond with ready will to the challenge of a genuine contemplative life. For such a person, he gives a programme for the journey towards poverty of spirit and liberation from self. In this context, *holy recollection* does not mean separation from external things but an internal solitude of spirit, an inner detachment from all that is not God. In an active sense, recollection means creating inner space for God. It does not mean less attention to obvious duties. The reference is rather to unnecessary items of thought or desire that have no bearing on our journey to God. To holy recollection St John adds *spiritual silence*, which seems to indicate a passive recollection. In this case, the temple of recollecton is already built for the soul in which to pray. As St Teresa says: "These people are sometimes in the castle before they have begun to think about God at all. I cannot say where they entered it or how they heard their Shepherd's call".[3]

Nakedness and poverty are words that occur frequently in the writings of St John of the Cross. They can be taken to refer specifically to detachment from heavenly goods, from spiritual consolations and divine favours of whatever kind. The aim is to create a disposition of soul that is open to God's gift of himself rather than to any of his wonderful created gifts. It applies particularly to the beginner in contemplation. If we take contemplation to mean the plenitude of God in his self-giving to the soul, then the precautions prescribe a corresponding emptiness or inner space for God: "the place where one enjoys the peaceful comfort of the Holy Spirit and reaches union with God". The target therefore is union with God as a result of freedom from obstacles and from self-love.

The programme is threefold because the obstacles are three-fold: the world, the flesh, and the devil. St John discusses them in the order: the world, which is easiest to deal with; the devil, by whom we are most easily deceived; and the flesh (selfishness), which is the last to yield. There are three precautions under each of these three headings.

THE WORLD

1 *Equal love and forgetfulness of all persons.*   The first precaution is directed against disordered or selfish love of persons, whether they are relatives or others. As a practical rule it may seem to be impossible. But it is a good guideline for a beginner's emotional involvement. It covers an important affective area where the fervent beginner might easily be deceived. St John himself loved his family tenderly, especially his brother Francis. All the saints loved their families and friends, their human relationships reflecting their union with God. But this state of perfect love did not come to them automatically. Natural love of relatives and friends has to be purified and perfected, just as love for God has to be purified and perfected. Any form of selfish love is an obstacle to union with God. St John's precaution excludes any inordinate love or worry about one's family or friends, something that does them no good and may be a lack of trust in God. Any form of useless preoccupation hinders contemplation. The aim is perfect love for others, less emotional satisfaction or distress, less useless involvement on our journey to union with God.

St John does not want us to love our relatives less or fail in our duty of friendship towards them. He does not neglect the Gospel precept in order to focus on the perfection of the individual. His words are clear:

> Regard all as strangers, and *you will better fulfil your duty toward them* than by giving them the affection you owe God. Do not think about others, neither good things nor bad . . . And if you should wish to allow yourself some freedom in this matter, the devil will deceive you in one way or another, or you will deceive yourself under some color of good or of evil.[4]

The aim of the precaution is to preserve the beginner from an unreal world of petty friendships that breed tattered social relationships and preoccupation about apparent wrongs or injustices. It also confronts the beginner with the uncomfortable truth that we must sometimes please people less in order to love them more. "We must sometimes disappoint the world in order to save it, as Christ did."[5]

2 *Temporal Goods.* The goal here is silence and peace in the senses. The obstacle comes from possessions of any kind: food, clothing, accommodation, or personal comfort. When any of these good things becomes a preoccupation, taking in the mind the place that God should have, then detachment or penitential willingness to "go without" is required. St John's mnemonic here is: He who looks after the beasts will not forget you.

Sometimes in the case of fervent beginners, detachment itself becomes a preoccupation, a kind of uneasy anxiety to go without comfort. This might be a failure to break through to a healthy indifference and freedom from excessive self-consideration. A restless desire to be the perfect servant of God is less Christian than a true spirit of childhood, a practical trust in God and abandonment to his providence.

3 *Community Relationships.* The contemplative life requires strong personal decision. The precaution here is to preserve a certain independence on social issues. From the very beginning keep clear of taking sides. Now that you have learned something about the perfection of religious life, see that you do not apply this forthwith to the situation in which you live. Do not become a judge in Israel too soon.

> Many by not observing this not only have lost the peace and good of their soul, but have fallen and ordinarily continue to fall into many evils and sins. Never be scandalized or astonished at anything you happen to see or learn of, endeavoring to preserve your soul in forgetfulness of all that. For, should you desire to pay heed to things, many will seem wrong, even though you live among angels, because of your not understanding the nature of them . . .
>
> And if you do not guard yourself, acting as though you were not in the house, you will be unable to be a religious no matter how much you do, nor will you attain holy denudation and recollection, nor free yourself of the harm arising from these thoughts. If you are not cautious in this manner, the devil will catch you in one way or another. And you are already fully captive when you allow yourself distractions of this sort.[6]

The demand made by St John in this precaution may seem to be excessive. Undoubtedly he had his reasons for it. Perhaps because moral prescriptions are not of much practical use unless they are absolute. Perhaps his own experience of community life showed him the extent of the damage that can result from good-willed but misguided interference. Perhaps the precaution was dictated by the eremitical spirit of Carmel and its totality of self-giving. It is well known that great master musicians and painters submit their pupils to a rigorous discipline with a view to perfect freedom of performance in later years. Likewise St John of the Cross, the great spiritual master of liberty of spirit, makes what appears to be an excessive demand. He knew from experience the demands that should be made with a view to perfect union with God.

THE DEVIL

St John introduces these three precautions by observing that the most common ruse of Satan is to deceive spiritual persons by the appearance of good rather than of evil. He knows they will not choose a recognized evil. "Thus you should always be suspicious of what appears good, especially when not obliged by obedience." The three precautions are therefore arranged in view of God's redemptive plan, to which we adhere by obedience and humility.

1 *God's redemptive plan.* Apart from the obligations of your state of life, never take upon yourself any work that is not ordered by obedience, however good and full of charity that work may seem, whether for yourself or for anyone else inside or outside the house. The actions of a religious are not his own to dispose of. He has inserted himself into God's plan by vow. So he has to be cautious about indiscreet zeal and must exercise moderation in works of supererogation.

2 *The obedience of faith.* The devil does not understand God's loving plan in our regard. But, as the enemy of our good, he is a great meddler in the area of obedience. He tries to condition us psychologically so that we become victims of an attitude towards authority that makes obedience unusually difficult or, on the contrary, so easy that it ceases to be supernatural.
St John's precaution is directed towards personal liberation:

Watch, therefore, with singular care that you study neither his (the superior's) character, his mode of behavior, his ability, or any of his other methods of procedure, for you will so harm yourself as to change your obedience from divine to human, being motivated only by the visible traits of the superior, and not by the invisible God Whom you serve through him.[7]

Nowadays there is a strong bias against humble submission, as if it were the evidence of a servile spirit. As in all other areas, the corrective model here has to be Christ who took the form of a servant. "And being found in human form he humbled himself and became obedient unto death, even death on a cross." (Philippians 2:8) What we honour in obedience is God's loving plan, which we accept in faith as it is made known to us through others, whether that means the Rule, or the community, or the individual superior. The wish of a superior can be a secondary norm for us in God's design. Not that superiors have infallible knowledge of the divine will, they must search for it in faith, and they can be helped in this search by the community or by individual members. Even the great St Paul, after his Damascus experience, had to have his vision authenticated and his eyes opened by Ananias, a person of much less importance than himself in the divine plan.

3 *Humility.*   St Teresa referred to humility as the ointment of all our wounds. St John of the Cross proposes it in this precaution as the secret of happiness as well as the great barrier to Satan's interference. "Ever seek with all your heart to humble yourself in word and deed, rejoicing in the good of others as if it were your own, desiring that they be given precedence over you in all things, and this you should do wholeheartedly. You will thereby overcome evil with good, banish the devil, and possess a happy heart."[8]

THE FLESH

1 *Sensitivity* has the advantage of bringing with it a finer perception of spiritual values. But, like a too sensitive instrument, it can pick up also some troublesome interferences which might play upon a person's mood and lead to a distorted judgement. In three brief precautions, St John advises us to direct our spiritual life by *mind* rather than by *mood*. He is thinking of times of aridity when God ceases to nourish the soul through its feelings in favour of a more substantial food. In the first precaution he regards community life as a providential arrangement for God's activity during the passive night. Community life is a training ground, a school of perfection "that all may fashion and try you". The beginner is expected to have enough faith at this stage to see God's hand at work and to welcome his intervention.

The first precaution is to understand that you have come to the monastery so that all may fashion and try you ... Some will fashion you with words, others by deeds, and others with thoughts against you; and (that) in all this you must be submissive as is the statue to the craftsman who moulds it, to the artist who paints it, and to the gilder who embellishes it. If you fail to observe this precaution, you will not know how to overcome your sensitiveness and feelings, nor will you get along well in the community with the religious, nor attain holy peace, nor free yourself from many stumbling blocks and evils.[9]

2 *Constancy in times of crisis.* When the wine from the senses fails, keep your original purpose in view, realizing that motivation from any form of self-love, even what appears to be spiritual, has to be purified. It is a case of "wait and see" that the Lord is good.

3 In this final precaution, the soul is no longer on the defence against its moods. It is exhorted rather to *seek what is distasteful and arduous* in its spiritual exercises. The senses are concrete and particular. They confine the spirit which, although it needs nourishment from the senses, pines for something the senses cannot provide. The spirit is at home only in the open, universal realm. Aridity liberates the spirit from the restrictions of sense, and so St John ends his precautions on this note of liberation:

> The third precaution is that the interior man should never fix his eyes upon the pleasant feelings found in his spiritual exercises, becoming attached to them and carrying out these practices only for the sake of this satisfaction. Nor should he run from the bitterness he may find in them, but rather seek the arduous and distasteful and embrace it. By this practice the senses are held in check; without it, you will never lose self-love nor gain the love of God.[10]

NOTES

1 *The Sign of Jonas*, Journal, 20 March 1947, New York, Doubleday and Co. Inc., 1956, Image Books, p. 40
See also *Counsels of Light and Love of St John of the Cross*, introduction by Thomas Merton, London, Burns and Oates, 1977
2 *Precautions* 1, *K.*, p. 656
3 *Interior Castle* IV Mansions 3/3
4 *Precautions* 6, *K.*, p. 657
5 Brother Conchuir, *Religious Life Review*, July–August 1984, p. 181
6 *Precautions*, 8, 9, *K.*, p. 657, 658
7 *Precautions* 12, *K.*, p. 659
8 *Precautions* 13, *K.*, p. 660
9 *Precautions* 15, *K.*, p. 660
10 *Precautions* 17, *K.*, p. 661

6

PHASES OF
SPIRITUAL GROWTH

Very early in the Christian centuries different levels of perfection were recognized. Some people honoured God from fear, others with hope of reward, and others from a motive of perfect love. St Gregory of Nyssa distinguished those who avoid evil from fear of hell, those who do good in hope of heaven, and those who act only to please God and show him their love. This distinction of persons was later applied to phases of spiritual growth in the individual. St Augustine founded the steps of this growth on the virtue of charity. Charity, the essence of the spiritual life, has a gradual development. It is born, is nourished, and comes to maturity. So for Augustine, holiness is initial, developing, and perfect. St Thomas Aquinas followed this idea and distinguished beginners, who strengthen themselves in charity by destroying sin; proficients, who move forward by the exercise of the infused virtues; and the perfect, who adhere habitually to God by conforming their will to his. This was the division used by St John of the Cross in the three books of the *Ascent of Mount Carmel* and the two books of the *Dark Night*.

Souls begin to enter this dark night when God, gradually drawing them out of the state of *beginners* (those who practise meditation on the spiritual road), begins to place them in the state of *proficients* (those who are already contemplatives) so that by passing through this state they might reach that of the *perfect*, which is the divine union of the soul with God.[1]

PHASES OF SPIRITUAL GROWTH

	ACTIVE NIGHT		PASSIVE NIGHT		UNION
	OF SENSE	OF SPIRIT	OF SENSE	OF SPIRIT	
	ASCENT I	ASCENT II and III	DARK NIGHT I	DARK NIGHT II	SPIRITUAL CANTICLE / LIVING FLAME
	Mortification of the appetites (desires)	JOURNEY IN FAITH — Faith – Intellect, Hope – Memory, Charity – Will	God's communication to the soul		Spiritual Marriage / Spiritual Betrothal / Simple Union
			Purgation of vice	Purgation of roots of vice	
			Transition to Contemplation	*Transition to Union*	
	Death to sin	Life to God	Death to sin		Life to God
	(Baptism)	Theological life	(Confirmation)		(Eucharist)
MAN in captivity to sin	Good moral life	Lives to God	obscure beginnings of the mystical life		mystical life proper
lives to eat	eats to live				GOD

In a treatise called *De Triplici Via*, St Bonaventure favoured another terminology taken from the mystical writings of pseudo-Denys. The distinction of the three ways here is deduced from the different reactions of the soul, corresponding to God's ways of dealing with it. Thus we have the *Purgative Way* in which the mind disposes itself to receive the wisdom of God by removing itself from sin and imperfection; the *Illuminative Way*, in which it is fired with love because of meditation on revealed truth; and the *Unitive Way*, when it is enlightened directly by God.

This terminology of the three Ways was used by St John of the Cross at the beginning of his commentary on the *Spiritual Canticle*. As a division, it should cause little trouble to the reader, for its function in the commentary is minimal. The construction of a mystical treatise has to follow the logic of love rather than a neat arrangement of concepts. What the reader of the *Canticle* has to keep in mind is not a neat diversion but the dynamism of a love that moves the soul forward to the spiritual espousal (illuminative way) and to the mystical marriage (unitive way). The initial impetus for this movement is a wound of love, a very painful "absence" of God, which impels the soul to go out of self in search of the Beloved.

In the books of the *Ascent-Night*, on the contrary, division is important. In different parts of these commentaries St John is addressing different persons. "In each of these books the reader must keep in mind the intention we have in writing. Failure to do so will give rise to many doubts about what he reads."[2] The phases of spiritual growth in St John of the Cross are not numerous, but we need to be clear which phase or what kind of person he addresses in any particular context.

Repentance is frequently the beginning of spiritual growth, and repentant love may continue with a person to the end. Sometimes a careless person with little regard for God's law or spiritual values may unexpectedly become aware of his or her true condition in God's sight. This brings about a profound change of attitude and a new judgement of values under the light of God's holiness. St John of the Cross does not deal with this crisis of first conversion. He presupposes it and explains how God treats the soul *"after it has been resolutely converted* to His service". A resolute conversion may give the beginner a feeling of strength in the things of God. For St John, spiritual strength is judged by firmly rooted habits of virtue, "and since these persons have not had time to acquire those firm habits, their work must of necessity be feeble, like that of weak children",[3] and God acts with them accordingly.

> The grace of God acts just like a loving mother by re-engendering in the soul new enthusiasm and fervor in the service of God. With no effort on the soul's part, this grace causes it to taste sweet and delectable milk and to experience intense satisfaction in the performance of spiritual exercises, because God is handing the breast of His tender love to the soul, just as if it were a delicate child.
>
> The soul finds its joy, therefore, in spending lengthy periods at prayer, perhaps even entire nights; its penances are pleasures; its fasts, happiness; and the sacraments and spiritual conversations are its consolations.[4]

In St John's terminology, this person is a beginner. If there is to be further growth, perseverance in the virtues will be required, leading to another kind of conversion. The soul will now have to deny itself or God will deny it all sense pleasure in spiritual things. This will be the crisis of the night of sense. It will be passive insofar as God no longer gives "the breast of his tender love" to the soul, thus causing aridity or lack of pleasure in spiritual exercises. It will be active insofar as the soul itself will have to practise detachment from good things as well as bad, and remain content to go without sense satisfaction in practices that lead to God. The soul will have to detach itself from the very things that formerly were of spiritual benefit. This will be puzzling at first and the soul will have a natural tendency to continue with original methods that have now become obstacles. Through the crisis of the night of sense the beginner will pass on to the state of proficient and experience the beginnings of contemplation. The soul has now come to terms with aridity, discovering in it an unexpected form of the divine presence. This is the beginning of the illuminative way in which the soul spends many peaceful years and moves forward towards union with God. In some cases – St John says they are few – God brings the proficient to the state of the perfect by means of another crisis of growth, the night of the spirit. The change here is transformation rather than conversion. The soul's activities of knowledge and love are so "divinized" that they become one with the knowledge and love of God himself.

The night of spirit also has its active and passive phases. During this night the soul has to deny itself the things of the spirit, just as in the night of sense it had to deny itself the things of sense. To deny oneself the things of the spirit means to choose God himself in preference to all his gifts. The fact that something comes from God and is ordained by God for our spiritual advancement does not mean that it should become an object of attachment in preference to God. Normally, when St John is addressing the "spiritual man" he means one who is moving from the beginnings of obscure contemplation to perfect union with God. In *Ascent* Books II and III he shows how the spiritual person becomes the "divinized" or transformed person *actively* by the practice of "divine" virtues, faith in the intellect, hope in the memory, and love in the will. In *Dark Night* Book II he teaches how the transformation takes place *passively* by means of a dark and painful contemplation infused by God. This is a kind of divine anointing of the soul in its very depths, a radical healing of vice and imperfection. The soul does not know how this happens, but it afterwards discovers that it is on fire with a strong love. Nothing seems impossible to it in the service of God.

This burning love and fortitude are needed in the final stage of spiritual growth, union and transformation of the soul in God. St John brings out the intimacy of this union by the symbol of marriage; transformation is illustrated by the window and the ray of sunlight. Even in the highest state of union, the transformed soul remains distinct from God, just as the window remains distinct from the light. St John thus keeps clear of the pantheistic notions of union that were current in the pseudo-mysticism of his day.

> When God grants this supernatural favor to the soul, so great a union is caused that all the things of both God and the soul become one in participant transformation, and the soul appears to be God more than a soul. Indeed, it is God by participation. Yet truly, its being (even though transformed) is naturally as distinct from God's as it was before, just as the window, although illumined by the ray, has an existence distinct from the ray.[5]

Therefore, the final stage of spiritual growth (union and transformation in God) does not mean that the soul is absorbed in God so as to lose its identity. There may be an experience like that of absorption, but the soul remains itself and has to exercise its own activity, at least passively by its free consent. By yielding up its will to God it does not sign off its responsibility as a human being. Rather, it becomes more perfectly human and free because its will, united with God, participates in God's infinite freedom and perfection.

THE *ALUMBRADOS*

Interest in personal prayer flourished in the fervent spiritual climate of sixteenth-century Spain. The term *alumbrados* (the illumined) could originally be understood in a broad sense, embracing the orthodox *recogidos* (the "recollected") who tended to be members of religious orders and among whom were such writers as Osuna and Laredo; and the more heterodox *dejados*, (the "self-abandoned") who tended to be laity gathered around some "charismatic" individual. However, the term came to be applied more specifically to the less orthodox as early as 1525 when the Inquisition first took an interest in these groups, and particularly later in the second part of the century when

> the intense, illuminist fervour seen in some Franciscan monasteries and among some *beatas* (holy women) led to certain kinds of excesses as a result of which the term *alumbrado* . . . came to denote a person of pseudo-mystical, quietist tendencies.[6]

The basic flaw in the teaching of the *alumbrados* was the exaggerated importance they attached to mental prayer. They held that mental prayer was commanded by divine law and that by it all other precepts are fulfilled. Not even the celebration of the Eucharist, or obligations arising from charity, or obedience to lawful authority should be allowed to impede the exercise of mental prayer. The person at that time would be guided by the Holy Spirit directly and so would not have to obey any other law. Mental prayer accordingly was described as a kind of recollection in God's presence in which the mind does not engage in any movement of reasoning or reflection. There is no meditation properly so called, no reflection on images, on the Passion of Christ or on his humanity. By practice, the person would arrive at a state of perfection in which the faculties would be so submerged in God that they could no longer act in any way. This person would experience a certain ravishment of the Holy Spirit, an ecstasy of soul in which he or she would see the divine essence and behold the Trinity of Persons as the elect do in heaven. All the properties of beatitude would follow and the soul would be freed from the weakness incurred by original sin. Whatever it did would not be sin. Thus elevated, the soul would not be acting from choice but would be moved by the Holy Spirit. Obviously, this teaching could lead to all kinds of aberrations in the moral order. The investigations of the Inquisition provided several accounts of lapses of this kind.

St John of the Cross can often be heard as the voice of balance and wisdom over against the excesses of the Illuminists. He always speaks cautiously about any kind of special illumination of the Holy Spirit. People advanced in perfection may suppose that it is more pleasing to God to have guidance directly from heaven, since God sometimes grants their petition.

> Yet the truth is that, regardless of God's reply, such behavior is neither good nor pleasing to God. Rather He is displeased; not only displeased but frequently angered and deeply offended. The reason lies in the illicitness of transcending the natural boundaries God has established for the governing of creatures. He has fixed natural and rational limits by which man is to be ruled. A desire to transcend them, hence, is unlawful, and to desire to investigate and arrive at knowledge in a supernatural way is to go beyond the natural limits. It is unlawful, consequently, and God who is offended by everything illicit is displeased.[7]

The high point of illuminist teaching was its claim to have vision of the divine essence, to behold the Blessed Trinity on earth in the same way as the elect in heaven, thus implying an absolute certainty of being in the state of grace. This became the decisive norm for condemnation of heterodox mysticism. Although St John of the Cross deals with very exalted states of spirituality and recognizes very lofty experiences of God, he never removes these experiences from the order of faith.

It must be understood that if a person experiences some grand spiritual communication or feeling or knowledge, he should not think that his experiences are similar to the clear and essential vision or possession of God, or that the communication, no matter how remarkable it is, signifies a more notable possession of God or union with Him. It should be known too that if all these sensible and spiritual communications are wanting and a person lives in dryness, darkness, and dereliction, he must not thereby think that God is any more absent than in the former case. A person, actually, cannot have certain knowledge from the one state that he is in God's grace, nor from the other that he is not.[8]

Even in the highest stage of spiritual growth during the present life, one never becomes so "enlightened" as to pass beyond the order of faith. For faith respects the mystery of heavenly things while it gives us the possession of them. "If He comes to me I shall not see Him, and if He goes away I shall not understand." (Job 9:11)

NOTE ON ST JOHN'S SCHEME OF THE SPIRITUAL LIFE

The following simple diagram may help those who are not familiar with the terminology of St John of the Cross.

The heavy vertical line represents God's will to bring the soul straight to himself. The slender line to the left of it represents the human will coming gradually into conformity with the will of God. The beginner, whose form of prayer is meditation,

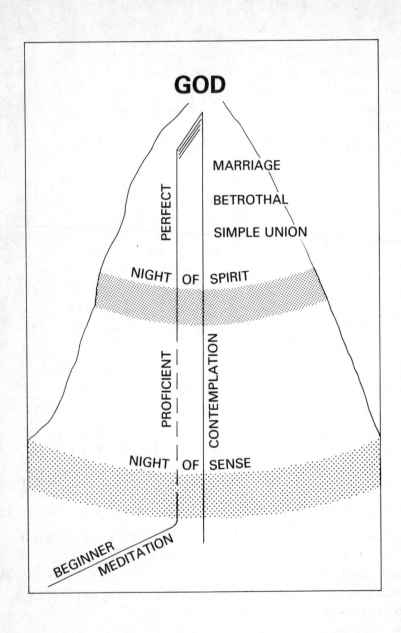

approaches the mountain and experiences a first crisis of growth with the night of sense. This night changes the beginner to the state of the proficient. The prayer of the proficient is contemplation, and with this the climb of the mountain really begins. The proficient has to live with no other support than the theological virtues, especially faith. The proficient is thus freed from dependence on anything like sensible consolation as a source of happiness, and is therefore sometimes referred to by St John of the Cross as the "spiritual" person. The will of the proficient is aligned to the will of God, though not perfectly (as the dotted line indicates). After a number of years as proficient, another crisis of growth may occur. The "spiritual" person may now be brought by God through the night of the spirit, and thus be raised to the state of the perfect. In this state the will of the soul is in complete conformity with the will of God. This is the goal of the mountain climb, as the soul reaches union with God. At first, it is "simple union", that is, union without further qualification. Afterwards it becomes betrothal, and finally the state of spiritual marriage.

> In the state of divine union a man's will is so completely transformed in God's will that it excludes anything contrary to God's will, and in all and through all is motivated by the will of God. Here we have the reason for stating that two wills become one. And this one will is God's will which becomes also the soul's. (I *Ascent* 11/2, 3, *K.*, p. 96)

The diagram given here differs from St John's sketch of Mount Carmel (*K.*, p. 66), where he is concerned chiefly to show the path of detachment to be followed in the active night, which leads directly to God, compared with the paths of attachment which do not reach the summit.

7

THE SIGNS OF
CONTEMPLATION

The exaggerated importance which the *alumbrados* attached to mental prayer had repercussions in the schools. Theologians were divided into two groups. One group (the *letrados*) distrusted the enthusiasm for mental prayer because of the dangers of illuminism, especially its anti-hierarchical and visionary tendencies. In this group we find the names of some eminent theologians: Melchior Cano OP, Domingo Soto and Mancia of Corpus Christi, a theologian of the Council of Trent, all of them anti-feminists. Their thinking was based on actual cases condemned by the Inquisition. St Teresa lists their objections as she takes up the defence for women and for mental prayer:

> Yet again and again people will say to us: "It is dangerous", "So-and-so was lost through doing this", "Someone else got into wrong ways", "Some other person, who was always praying, fell just the same", "It is bad for virtue", "It is not meant for women; it may lead them into delusions", "They would do better to stick to their spinning", "These subtleties are of no use to them", "It is quite enough for them to say their Paternoster and Ave Maria".[1]

With this last remark St Teresa was in full agreement. She accepted the challenge by devoting half of her *Way of Perfection* to a consideration of the Paternoster showing how, when properly recited, it can lead to the highest contemplation. Though she distinguished vocal and mental prayer, she found no separation between them, for if it is prayer at all the mind must have part in it. In order to make vocal prayer well, a person would have to spend time first in mental prayer, considering to Whom our prayer is addressed and who we ourselves are.

The second group of theologians (the *espirituales*) preached and practised mental prayer. They were Luis of Granada, John of Avila, Peter of Alcantara, Francis Borgia, and others. For them, mental prayer was its own justification. It could not be judged by systematic or scientific theologians. St Teresa disagreed with them, and gave her "little book on prayer" (*The Way of Perfection*) to one of the *letrados* (Garcia of Toledo) for correction. She was convinced that Christian prayer must have its foundation in revealed truth. Those who studied this truth were competent to decide on its various modes of expression. They could test the foundations of her prayer and judge the orthodoxy of her writings.

The fundamental truth of revelation is the love God has manifested in his Son and the friendship and intimacy he desires to have with us. Thus for St Teresa the degrees of prayer are degrees of friendship, contemplation being the gift of a special kind of divine intimacy, leading ultimately to spiritual marriage with Christ, the heavenly Bridegroom. Accordingly, she formulated her famous definition of mental prayer as "an intimate sharing between friends; it means taking time frequently to be alone with Him who we know loves us".[2] This beautiful definition is wider than what we usually think of as "meditation", from which St Teresa seems to distinguish it, for she regards meditation as the road to the virtues, mental prayer as requiring the virtues, and contemplation as requiring the "greatest virtues". Her insistence on the virtues comes from the fact that virtue, as a habit of the mind, is a kind of second nature and so it determines the quality of persons. Virtue has to be crowned by love, "the form of the other virtues", for charity makes the other virtues to be forms of love.[3] Hence perfect virtue, implying perfect love, indicates the kind of person capable of that intimate divine friendship given in contemplation. St Teresa admits that God is sometimes pleased to show favour to people who are in an evil state: "But I cannot believe that He would grant them contemplation. For that is a divine union, in which the Lord takes His delight in the soul and the soul takes its delight in Him".[4]

Since it normally takes some time for friendship to develop into an intimate relationship, St Teresa holds out no promise of instant contemplation, nor does she provide any technique for becoming a contemplative. She exhorts us instead to become the kind of person that God would be able to take for his friend. This has to be God's gift, since even the "greatest virtues" could not purchase the friendship of the King of glory. And so contemplation has to be a free gift, though it is part of St Teresa's teaching that God never fails to repay anyone who has taken him for a friend.[5] When the nuns of St Joseph's, Avila, asked her if they could rightly desire this gift, she gave three answers: strive for the great virtues rather than for the great favours; humility sees and accepts its place in God's plan; and contemplation is given with a view to the cross. Sharing of sorrows has a unique role to play in the development of intimacy. Only a trusted friend is chosen to share a burden. What better sign of friendship could God give?

To suppose that He would admit to His close friendship pleasure-loving people who are free from all trials is ridiculous. I feel quite sure that God gives them much greater trials: and that He leads them by a hard and rugged road, so that they sometimes think they are lost and will have to go back and begin again. Then His Majesty is obliged to give them sustenance – not water, but wine, so that they may become inebriated by it and not realize what they are going through and what they are capable of bearing. Thus I find few true contemplatives who are not courageous and resolute in suffering; for, if they are weak, the first thing the Lord does is to give them courage so that they may fear no trials that may come to them.

I think, when those who lead an active life occasionally see contemplatives receiving consolations, they suppose that they never experience anything else. But I can assure you that you might not be able to endure their sufferings for as long as a day. The point is that the Lord knows everyone as he really is and gives each his work to do – accordingly to what He sees to be most fitting for his soul, and for His own Self, and for the good of his neighbour.[6]

In St Teresa's writings the word "contemplation" usually means clear contemplation, with the consolations and happiness that accompany it. When she calls it "supernatural" she means something over and above the ordinary workings of grace, not just the supernatural root of contemplation in theological virtue. St John of the Cross, on the other hand, extends the term "contemplation" to include an initial obscure phase. There was need for him therefore to give some signs when this dark contemplation begins and what the conduct of the soul should be at this time.

Actually, at the beginning of this state the loving knowledge is almost unnoticeable. There are two reasons for this: first, ordinarily the incipient loving knowledge is extremely subtle and delicate, and almost imperceptible; second, a person who is habituated to the exercise of meditation, which is wholly sensible, hardly perceives or feels this new insensible, purely spiritual experience.[7]

St John has given two sets of signs; one for recognizing when discursive meditation should be discontinued (II *A.*, 13), the other for discerning if the night of sense, that is, initial purgative contemplation has begun (I *D.N.*, 9). The first set of three signs occurs when St John is discussing the beginnings of the active night of spirit, so that the "spiritual" person may know if the time has come to discontinue meditation:

> The first is the realization that one cannot make discursive meditation nor receive satisfaction from it as before. The second sign is an awareness of a disinclination to fix the imagination or sense faculties upon other particular objects, exterior or interior. The third and surest sign is that a person likes to remain alone in loving awareness of God, without particular considerations, in interior peace and quiet and repose, and without the acts and exercises (at least discursive, those in which one progresses from point to point) of the intellect, memory and will, and that he prefers to remain only in the general, loving awareness and knowledge we mentioned, without any particular knowledge or understanding.[8]

The only positive sign, the third, is the surest, because it is really a description of initial contemplation. Friends who have become intimate like to be alone. They do not need to meditate beforehand what they are going to say to each other. If God is now the soul's intimate friend, contemplation will mean being lost in admiration of his wonderful Being and of the unlimited goodness revealed in his eternal plan of salvation. Because the Creator of all things is universal, unlimited Good, the soul will not feel attracted by other particular goods, but will want to rest in this general, loving awareness of its Friend, who is beyond the grasp of any particular knowledge.

The second set of signs occurs in the discussion of the passive night of sense. Since the passive night presupposes the presence of contemplation already at work in the soul, this set has no positive sign. The three signs here are no more than a check on the symptoms, in order to rule out sin or imperfection, tepidity or lukewarmness, ill health or "any bad humor". The signs listed here are: no satisfaction in creatures, powerlessness to meditate as formerly, and an anxious care about pleasing God in all things, which is obviously an indication of love, even if not a positive sign of contemplation.

With the gift of contemplation, in St Teresa's language, the kingdom of God has come in the soul. A divine work has begun. But it is not a one-sided event. It is a call as well as a gift. It is part of the universal dialogue of salvation, and the divine work can be frustrated if the privileged person does not receive the kingdom as a child, that is, as receiver rather than as agent. The conduct of the soul during prayer has to change from actively striving after concepts and images to the receiving of what is now being given. The issue is important because of the divine work to be accomplished. This explains why so much notice has been taken of this beginning stage of contemplation and of the signs that accompany it. St John gives some reasons why a change of tactics must now take place, explaining how the desire to work with the faculties would hinder rather than help the divine action in the soul:

The reason is that now in this state of contemplation, when the soul has left discursive meditation and entered the state of proficients, it is God who works in it. He therefore binds the interior faculties and leaves no support in the intellect, nor satisfaction in the will, nor remembrance in the memory. At this time a person's own efforts are of no avail, but an obstacle to the interior peace and work God is producing in the spirit through that dryness of sense. Since this peace is something spiritual and delicate, its fruit is quiet, delicate, solitary, satisfying, and peaceful, and far removed from all these other gratifications of beginners, which are very palpable and sensory.[9]

Prayer at this stage is a sharing between friends even more than it was before. Two personal freedoms are engaged in the exchange of love. The created freedom is now exercised more directly with God himself than with choosing motives for loving him.

THE ROLES OF MIND AND IMAGINATION IN PRAYER

The first Christian spiritual writer to discuss the roles of the mind and imagination in prayer was Evagrius Ponticus (AD 346–399). He has been described as "the founder of monastic mysticism and the most fertile and interesting spiritual author of the Egyptian desert".[10] He was a protégé of the great Cappadocians, Basil and the two Gregorys, and was renowned particularly for his writings on prayer. These would not have been known in sixteenth-century Spain but he had exercised a strong influence on Western thought through such writers as John Cassian, and pseudo-Denys. Evagrius advocated imageless, conceptless prayer for two reasons. One was that in order to pray the mind needs to be free from anxieties about worldly business, from images arising from unquieted passions, and even from innocent but irrelevant thoughts. "You will not be able to pray purely if you are all involved with material affairs and agitated with unremitting concerns. For prayer is a rejection of concepts."[11] The other reason is that God is beyond all images of him that the mind can form:

When you are praying do not fancy the Divinity like some image formed within yourself. Avoid also allowing your spirit (*nous*, mind) to be impressed with the seal of some particular

65

shape, but rather, free from all matter, draw near the immaterial Being and you will attain to understanding.[12]

In short,

strive to render your mind deaf and dumb at the time of prayer and then you will be able to pray.[13]

This kind of language continued down the centuries. Through writers like Francis of Osuna and Bernardino of Laredo it reached St Teresa and St John of the Cross in the form of a question: whether a person should think of nothing in prayer as a preparation for contemplation?[14] "To think of nothing" (*no pensar nada*) became a bone of contention among spiritual masters in sixteenth-century Spain. St Teresa had read Osuna's *Third Spiritual Alphabet* when she was twenty-two. It taught her the prayer of recollection and led her on to the prayer of quiet. Twenty years later, at the time of her second conversion, she was reading the *Ascent of Mount Sion*, in which there is a chapter (27) entitled "What is meant by thinking of nothing in perfect contemplation?". The author (Laredo) holds that "in the secret pursuit of this business" no thoughts, however good, should be allowed to enter the way of quiet in perfect contemplation. To think of nothing in prayer is not proposed as an exercise for beginners but for those who, from long practice, can "stay their mind" on love alone. Laredo's interpretation of it presupposes a certain maturity:

In this thinking of nothing there is comprehended a great world, wherein perfect contemplation comprehends and holds within itself all that merits being desired, and as this "all" is God alone, it follows that in His presence all else is nothing; and being nothing, is no subject for thought.

Quiet contemplation occupies itself in God alone – and by this I mean in His love alone. The soul that contemplates Him thus is aware of nought within itself save the spark of love, which is most living within it.[15]

St Teresa gives very positive guidance on this debated question. Although it is true that, from the abundance of knowledge given in contemplation, the ordinary working of the faculties used in meditation is impeded, the soul must never do this itself in order to produce contemplation. At no stage in the life of prayer is there question of doing absolutely nothing. As she says when treating of the Prayer of Quiet,

> if His Majesty has not begun to grant us absorption, I cannot understand how we can cease thinking in any way which will not bring us more harm than profit, although this has been a matter of continual discussion among spiritual persons.[16]

She did not advise suspending thought unless the soul were in possession of an alternative given by God. She was very much opposed to suppressing the activity of the mind, for the simple reason that dryness would then increase and the imagination become more restless than before.

According to St John's teaching, it is normally only after long perseverance in meditation that love and knowledge coalesce in a state of loving awareness of God. Because of the capital of knowledge thus acquired over a period of time, the soul does not now need to search out motives or reasons for love, and so it can remain in that simple, general awareness of God without the labour of meditation.

It should be known that the purpose of discursive meditation on divine subjects is the acquisition of some knowledge and love of God. Each time a person through meditation procures some of this knowledge and love he does so by an act. Many acts, in no matter what area, will engender a habit. Similarly, the repetition of many particular acts of this loving knowledge becomes so continuous that a habit is formed in the soul. God, too, effects this habit in many souls, without the precedence of at least many of these acts as means, by placing them at once in contemplation.

What the soul, therefore, was periodically acquiring through the labor of meditation on particular ideas has now, as we said, been converted into the habitual and substantial, general and loving knowledge. This knowledge is neither distinct nor particular, as the previous. Accordingly the moment prayer begins, the soul, as one with a store of water, drinks peaceably, without the labor and need of fetching the water through the channels of past considerations, forms, and figures. At the moment it recollects itself in the presence of God, it enters upon an act of general, loving, peaceful, and tranquil knowledge, drinking wisdom and love and delight.[17]

Thought therefore is not suppressed during contemplation, but meditation on particular ideas has been converted into an habitual, general, loving knowledge. This knowledge resides in the passive intellect. The distinction between "passive" and "active" intellect was used by St John of the Cross to explain the nature of infused contemplation. According to the scholastics, the intellect, like the human eye, is passive. It receives whatever is presented to it. It is "informed" by its object, which is the active agent in the birth of knowledge. The human intellect is a purely immaterial faculty but it normally receives the objects of its knowledge through bodily activity. For this work, the scholastics postulated another faculty, the active or agent intellect. This active or messenger intellect goes to the imagination for the forms of things to be understood. This is the faculty employed in meditation. St John says that the active intellect goes to the imagination and fantasy "as though to a seaport or market to buy and sell provisions".[18] What the active intellect brings home to the passive intellect retains always some connotation of its origin. It is labelled, as it were, and has a name, and can be spoken about. In the case of infused contemplation, on the other hand, a person receives God-given knowledge and love that has somehow bypassed the working of the active intellect. This new kind of knowledge has not come through the usual channel of imagination and fantasy. It carries no label of origin, has no name, and is therefore ineffable. Since God bypasses the active intellect during contemplation, this active power and the work of discursive meditation should remain quiet so as not to hinder the divine working. In that sense, a person should "think of nothing" during contemplation. But the mind is not blank. It has instead a new kind of awareness which St John calls substantial knowledge. What we receive through meditation comes to the intellect like paper-wrapped goods from the market of the imagination. When God gives "substantial knowledge" directly there are no accidental wrappings to be admired and we may be at a loss without them.

> In contemplation God teaches the soul very quietly and secretly, without its knowing how, without the sound of words, and without the help of any bodily or spiritual faculty, in silence and quietude, in darkness to all sensory and natural things. Some persons call this contemplation knowing by unknowing. For this knowledge is not produced by the intellect which the philosophers call the agent intellect, which works upon forms, phantasies, and apprehensions of the corporal faculties; rather it is produced in the possible or passive intellect. This possible intellect, without the reception of these forms, etc., receives passively only substantial knowledge, which is divested of images and given without any work or active function of the intellect.[19]

This substantial knowledge is more enjoyable than all other

things, because without the soul's labour, it affords peace and rest, relish and delight. Accordingly, a person should not mind if his or her accustomed meditation fails. This in fact is desirable lest the mind's own activity become an obstacle to the infused gift of contemplation. Thus the gift will be received in greater plenitude and the enkindling of love become more ardent. For contemplation is nothing else than a secret, peaceful, loving inflow of God, which if not hampered fires the soul with a spirit of love.

The question naturally arises: Are proficients, because they are beginning to experience contemplation, never again to practise meditation? It is not St John's intention that meditation should be given up so abruptly. In the beginning, the habit of contemplation is not so perfect that a person can engage in it at will, and the exercise of meditation may still be possible. Certainly, the soul will often experience this loving, peaceful awareness passively without having begun to meditate. But frequently a gentle and moderate use of meditation will be necessary in order to enter this state. But once the soul is placed in it, the activity of the faculties ceases. St John qualifies this by adding:

> It is affirmed that the person does nothing, not because he fails to understand, but because he understands by dint of no effort other than the reception of what is bestowed.[20]

This may be taken as St John's verdict on the *no pensar nada*. Far from being blank, the mind receives God's communication in loving awareness.

> It is more exact to say that then the work is done in the soul and the knowledge and delight is already produced, than that the soul does anything, besides attentively loving God and refraining from the desire to feel or see anything. In this loving

awareness the soul receives God's communication passively, just as a man, without doing anything else but keep his eyes open, receives light passively. This reception of the light infused supernaturally into the soul is a passive knowing.[21]

The proximate disposition, therefore, for infused contemplation is the loving awareness of the attentive mind, not the suppression of its act. This loving attention is the fruit of former, long-continued meditation. It may be called an intermediate stage between meditation and contemplation, a kind of launching stage for passive prayer. At this stage, a person is expected to be very free and detached from all desire for spiritual experience, taste, or feeling. He or she must "let go" all attraction for the natural, human mode of working during prayer, content to remain in solitude of soul and openness to God. Ultimately, even the loving attention of this transition stage may have to be "let go" in favour of a new phase of infused divine wisdom.

When it happens, therefore, that a person is conscious in this manner of being placed in solitude and in the state of listening, he should even forget the practice of loving attentiveness I mentioned so as to remain free for what the Lord then desires of him. He should make use of that loving awareness only when he does not feel himself placed in this solitude, or inner idleness or oblivion or spiritual listening. That he may recognize it, it always comes to pass with a certain peace and calm and inward absorption.[22]

There will be many readers of this chapter who have been wondering where they fit in. Although they are attracted to contemplative prayer they do not seem to have come by the route that has been described. They have rarely practised or have never really enjoyed any real form of regular discursive meditation. In fact, it is not unusual for people to be attracted to a simple form of prayer early on. In their case, prayer still needs to develop towards contemplation, and the function that is performed by meditation has to be supplied in some other way, through study of the Bible, through spiritual reading, through discussion, etc. For them, in the night of sense, all these things may lose their former excitement, and have to be rediscovered in a new and deeper way after a period of aridity.

Some other readers will have learned an imaginative method of meditation on scenes in the life of Christ, more free than the strictly discursive methods, and they may come to contemplative prayer through a gradual simplification, or they may find that their imagination suddenly refuses to work in its former way. Some may continue with a mixture of silence and simple meditation, the two complementing each other.

Whatever way people have come, growth in friendship with God and growth in prayer continue. As St Teresa says, God and the soul get to know each other. There is no longer need for an elaborate introduction. A prayer of loving attention will be the outcome of the soul's fidelity and perseverence. At times the soul may feel that it is idle during prayer, becuse the more perfect this loving awareness becomes the less perceptible it is. Nevertheless, any general, loving awareness of God during prayer is a full occupation for the mind. Faith and charity are thus reaching their perfect state as theological virtues. The prayer that results is what St John described as "loving attention" or "the simple gaze of love". St Teresa called it the "prayer of recollection", following Osuna and the Franciscan tradition. It was after the time of St John of the Cross that it came to be known as "acquired contemplation", and the Carmelites accepted the name as representing St John's mind. The difference between acquired and infused contemplation lies in the greater abundance of "the spirit of divine wisdom" infused, and also the fact of discontinuity with what went before. Acquired contemplation is a development that can be traced. Infused contemplation is a surprise gift.

> This wisdom is loving, tranquil, solitary, peaceful, mild, and an inebriator of the spirit, by which the soul feels tenderly and gently wounded and carried away, without knowing by whom, nor from where, nor how. The reason is that this wisdom is communicated without the soul's own activity.[23]

NOTES

1   St Teresa *Way of Perfection*, 21/2, Complete Works, translated by E. Allison Peers, The New Ark Library, Sheed & Ward, 1963, vol. II, p. 89

2   St Teresa *The Book of her Life*, Ch. 8/5 Kavanaugh-Rodriguez translation: The Collected Works of St Teresa of Avila, Washington, D.C., ICS publications, 1976, vol. I, p. 67

3   St Thomas Aquinas, *Summa Theologica*, translated by the Fathers of the English Dominican Province, Westminster, Maryland, Christian Classics, II II q 23 a 8 ad 1, vol. III, p. 1269

4   *Way of Perfection*, Op. cit., Ch. 16/6, vol. II, p. 65

5   *The Book of her Life*, Op. cit., Ch. 8/5, vol. I, p. 67

6   *Way of Perfection*, Op. cit., Ch. 18/3, vol. II, p. 73

7   II *A.*, 13/7, *K.*, p. 141

8   II *A.*, 13/2, 3, 4, *K.*, p. 140–1

9   I *D.N.*, 9/7, *K.*, p. 315

10   Johannes Quasten, *Patrology*, Westminster, Maryland, Christian Classics, 1983, vol. III, p. 169

11   Evagrius Ponticus, *The Praktikos and Chapters on Prayer*, translated with an introduction and notes by John Bamberger OCSO, Kalamazoo, Michigan, 1981, *Cistercian Studies Series* no. 4, ch. 70, p. 66

12   Ibid., Ch. 66, p. 66

13   Ibid., Ch. 11, p. 57

14   Francis of Osuna (*c.* 1492–1540) was Spanish and a member of the Observant (reformed) Franciscans, author of *The Third Spiritual*

Alphabet, translated and introduced by Mary E. Miles, London, Classics of Western Spirituality SPCK, 1981, Bernardino of Laredo (1482–1540) was a Spanish Franciscan lay Brother, medical doctor, author of *The Ascent of Mount Sion*, being the third book of the treatise of that name, translated with introduction and notes by E.A. Peers, London, Faber, 1952

15   *The Ascent of Mount Sion*, Ch. 27, p. 170
16   *Interior Castle*, IV Mansions Ch. 3/4, Peers trans., vol. II, p. 242
17   II *A.*, 14/2, *K.*, p. 142–3
18   II *A.*, 16/4, *K.*, p. 151
19   *Sp. Cant.*, stanza 39/12, *K.*, p. 561
20   II *A.*, 15/2, *K.*, p. 149
21   II *A.*, 15/2, *K.*, p. 148
22   *L.F.*, stanza 3/35, *K.*, p. 623
23   *L.F.*, stanza 3/38, *K.*, p. 625

N.B. For the origin of the name "acquired contemplation", and for the promotion of the prayer of "acquired" or "active" contemplation by the Carmelites after the time of St John of the Cross, see *St. John of the Cross* by Father Gabriel of St Mary Magdalen ODC, Cork, Mercier Press, 1946, pp. 181–4.

8

THE ACTIVE
NIGHT OF SENSE

This chapter is concerned with the first book of the *Ascent*, which is a commentary on the first stanza of the poem *One Dark Night* and deals with the active night of sense. The second and third books comment on the second stanza, and their subject is the active night of spirit. Thus the *Ascent* as a whole discusses our own active role in the purgation of sense and spirit. The passive purgation is discussed in the two books of the *Dark Night*, which St John at first called Book Four of the *Ascent*, making clear that the *Ascent* and the *Dark Night* are to be read as one treatise. In the *Living Flame* (st. I/25) he refers to "*The Dark Night of The Ascent of Mount Carmel*".

We can take the words "active purgation" to mean our ascetical preparation for reaching union with God. The first introductory sentence is a key to what follows: "This treatise explains how to reach divine union *quickly*". Of all St John's writings, *Ascent* I is probably the most challenging and, in some ways, the easiest to misunderstand. As on any journey, the aim is to unburden the soul of earthly things that weigh it down, to enable it to move along in the freedom of spirit necessary for divine union. The fervent beginner will brook no delay; and from the first glance at St John's instructions, there will be little room for compromise.

The stanzas of the poem are cited as a summary of the doctrine, as a basis "for all that I shall say". They describe the way that leads to the summit of the mount – "that high state of perfection which we here call union of the soul with God". The reader may be surprised to learn that the poem of the *Dark Night* is a "song of the soul's happiness". It is the love song of one who has arrived after climbing to the summit. The whole journey "toward that divine light of perfect union with God" is an enterprise of love. This is uppermost in St John's mind whenever he describes the trials of the night. "These are so numerous and profound that human science cannot understand them adequately; nor does experience of them equip one to explain them."[1] St John's teaching was not based only on experience, for it can "fail and deceive us". Though he sometimes made use of his experience to clarify certain aspects of his doctrine, he relied chiefly on Scripture and the teaching of the Church. His confidence in writing, he said, was in the Lord, who would enable him to present the doctrine "because it is extremely necessary to so many souls".[2]

God calls many people to perfect union with himself and desires to place them in this dark night, but they do not respond because firstly, they do not want to enter the night; secondly, they misunderstand themselves; thirdly, they are without "suitable and alert directors who will show them the way to the summit". The obstacle is not always a lack of effort. Many weary themselves with excessive effort, as if they would reach the summit on their own terms.

> They do not willingly adapt themselves to God's work of placing them on the pure and reliable road leading to union . . . Some souls, instead of abandoning themselves to God and cooperating with Him, hamper Him by their indiscreet activity or resistance.[3]

The purpose of St John's teaching, then, is to show both proficients and beginners "how to practice abandonment to

God's guidance when He wants them to advance".

> Some people – and it is sad to see them – work and tire themselves greatly, and yet go backwards; they look for perfection in exercises that are of no profit to them, but rather a hindrance. Others continue to make fine progress in peace and tranquillity. Some individuals encounter an encumbrance in the very consolation and favors God bestows on them for the sake of their advancement, and they advance not at all.[4]

It is a fatal error to start a career in life, or any new project with preconceived ideas. This is especially true of the spiritual life. A small error in the beginning, that is, some mistaken notion of what God wants from us, can lead to greater errors the farther we proceed. At the time of St John of the Cross, sanctity was considered to be an achievement brought off by great deeds and especially by great penitential exercises. But though God may give the grace of great deeds and great penance to certain souls called to this way of life, their sanctity does not consist in these; it consists rather in the fact that they go along with what God wants from them. Essentially, sanctity is God's loving work in the soul. By our response to this love we enter the dialogue of salvation. But if we persist in desiring something that God does not will, our love-response falters and we are not moving towards union with God, however insignificant that "something" may be. St John did not prescribe special prayers for the beginner, though he did recommend that the seven petitions of the Paternoster "be repeated often, and with fervor and with care. For in these, as I say, are embodied everything that is God's will and all that is fitting for us".[5] Neither did he prescribe special penances, though he chose a penitential life for himself. Instead, he wrote a number of chapters on the mortification of desires and appetites. Failure to go along with what God wants from us is the result of some disorder in our appetites. It is this disorder that St John wishes to correct when he speaks of "mortification of the appetites".

The appetites themselves are good, and our use of them brings us to God, provided we are free at heart. Detachment means freedom to move towards God without hindrance. Hearing, seeing, smelling, tasting, touching are unavoidable; "yet they will no more hinder a man – if he denies them – than if they were not experienced". This denial, sometimes referred to as nakedness or denudation of appetite, is called "night" for the soul.

> For we are not discussing the mere lack of things; this lack will not divest the soul, if it craves for these objects. We are dealing with the denudation of the soul's appetites and gratifications; this is what leaves it free and empty of all things, even though it possesses them. Since the things of the world cannot enter the soul, they are not in themselves an encumbrance or harm to it; rather, it is the will and appetite dwelling within it that causes the damage.[6]

Our greatest dignity as human beings is that we are *capaces Dei*, that is, we can have God in our mind and heart. If our heart wants nothing but God, we are living up to the full measure of that dignity. "For love effects a likeness between the lover and the object loved." St John shows at some length the vast distance there is between God and creatures, so that we might be persuaded to keep our desires up to the level of our true dignity, and not become enslaved. "He who loves a creature, then, is as low as that creature, and in some way even lower, because love not only equates, but even subjects the lover to the loved object." Hence a person subject to appetites will never attain "the royal freedom of spirit" that belongs to divine union. We have a choice between two kinds of freedom, the freedom to follow our appetites or the freedom of the Spirit of God. "All the sovereignty and freedom of the world compared with the freedom and sovereignty of the Spirit of God is utter slavery, anguish, and captivity." He who is attached to the freedom of his appetites "is considered and treated by God as a base slave and prisoner, not as a son. For such a one, the royal freedom of spirit attained in divine union is impossible, because freedom has nothing to do with slavery. And freedom cannot abide in a heart dominated by the appetites – in a slave's heart; it dwells in a liberated heart, which is a son's heart."[7]

St John is not an enemy of pleasure. He follows the teaching of St Paul: "You cannot belong to Christ unless you crucify all self-indulgent passions and desires" (Galatians 5). St John's thesis is that by satisfying selfish desire we deprive ourselves of the taste for true pleasure. He quotes the example of the manna in the desert, which contained the sweetness of every taste:

> Oh, if people knew how much spiritual good and abundance they lose by not attempting to raise their appetites above childish things, and if they knew to what extent, by not desiring the taste of these trifles, they would discover in this simple spiritual food the savor of them all.[8]

Frequently, it is not the simple statement of the doctrine that we need. We hesitate to enter the night because we misunderstand ourselves. We are not always conscious of the motives of our actions. Beneath many of our "holy decisions" there may lurk other subtle pressures. These may have the name of self-gratification in spiritual things, pride in self-perfection, preconceived notions of what the "correct" thing should be, or other pressures without an accepted name. These motives become clearer to us if our mortification of appetite becomes more habitual, our knowledge of God increasing also with our self-knowledge. That is why St John sees no let-up on a constant self-denial of our likes and dislikes. "The road and ascent to God, necessarily demands *a habitual effort* to renounce and mortify the appetites; the sooner this mortification is achieved, the sooner the soul reaches the top. But until the appetites are eliminated, a person will not arrive, no matter how much virtue he practices." With all the appetites mortified there comes a new knowledge and a new love of God.

> The soul will be clothed in God, in a new understanding of God (through the removal of the understanding of the old man), and in a new love of God in God – once the will is stripped of all the cravings and satisfactions of the old man. And God vests the soul with new knowledge when the other old ideas and images are cast aside. He causes all that is of the old man, the abilities of the natural being to cease, and attires all the faculties with new supernatural abilities. As a result a man's activities, once human, now become divine. This is achieved in the state of union where the soul in which God alone dwells has no other function than that of an altar, on which God is adored in praise and love.[9]

We can guess the importance that St John attached to this doctrine by the thoroughness with which he dealt with the subject. In five chapters he described how much harm the appetites can bring, pairing each defect for emphasis. Desire *wearies and tires* a person; *torments and afflicts*; *blinds and darkens*; *defiles and stains*; *weakens and makes lukewarm*. It saps the strength needed for perseverance in the practice of virtue. These chapters have been praised for their psychological insight. St John is interested primarily in the ascent of the soul to God. But the first phase of that ascent requires the right use of reason. Reason, not appetite, must be our guide. The second phase is the submission of reason to God. So the whole discourse on appetite is for the enthronement of reason, not without many scriptural references to a supernatural end. The problem at this stage of the spiritual life is, who has control in the house of the soul, mind or mood?

Pressure from habitual appetite causes a sickness of judgement. We value things according as we have them at heart, not as they are in truth. We are prisoners of desire. Being driven by mood does not always mean being driven to evil, but rather to an apparent good, since our reason is fettered by appetite in its discernment. St John laments this deficiency:

> The ignorance of some is extremely lamentable; they burden themselves with extraordinary penances and many other exercises, thinking these are sufficient for the attainment of union with the divine wisdom. But these practices are insufficient if a person does not diligently strive to deny his appetites. If these people would attempt to devote only a half of that energy to the renunciation of their desires, they would profit more in a month than in years with all these other exercises.[10]

It is only when appetites have developed that their destructive power is revealed. If they are not dealt with in the initial stage they soon take over, and "result in killing a man in his relationship with God". Even in less extreme cases, the harm done to the soul is serious. St John has a number of passages on the sad condition of the soul that is not yet liberated from tendencies that are unreasonable, and hurtful to spiritual progress.

> Even though they do not go to this extent, it is sad to consider the condition of the poor person in whom they dwell. How unhappy he is with himself, how cold toward his neighbors, how sluggish and slothful in the things of God. No illness makes walking as burdensome, or eating as distasteful, as do the appetites for creatures render the practice of virtue burdensome and saddening to a man. Ordinarily, the reason many people do not have diligence and eagerness for the acquisition of virtue is that their appetites and affections are not fixed purely on God.[11]

Having stated the doctrine on desires, St John seems to have been confronted with some further practical questions. Like the disciples, after our Lord's instruction, one might say: if this is the doctrine on desire, then who can be saved? "For it seems to be an extremely arduous task for a person to attain such purity and nakedness that he has no affection for anything."[12]

In reply to this query, St John makes a distinction between the voluntary appetites and the natural appetites. Nothing can come between us and God unless we have made some kind of decision about it. Natural appetites are not directly within the realm of our decision-making. They sometimes run their course independently of free choice, that is, independently of our exchange of love with God. Natural appetites therefore will not damage love, and this is St John's chief concern. "I am speaking of the voluntary appetites, because the natural ones are little or no hindrance at all to the attainment of union, provided they do not receive one's consent nor pass beyond the first movements in which the rational will plays no role. For to eradicate the natural appetites, that is, to mortify them entirely, is impossible in this life . . . It will even happen that while a person is experiencing an intense union of will in the prayer of quiet these appetites will be actually dwelling in his sensitive part – yet the superior part of his soul will be paying no attention to them."[13]

The guiding principle of St John's teaching is applied here to the desires: in the state of union a person's will is so completely transformed in God's will that it excludes anything contrary to what God wills. Therefore any freely willed desire for anything that is a sin or even only an imperfection, must be mortified – because it is when we give free assent to such a desire that it becomes a departure from love.

If anyone is to reach perfect union with God through his will and love, he must obviously first be freed from every appetite however slight. That is, he must not give the consent of his will knowingly to an imperfection, and he must have the power and freedom to be able, upon advertence, to refuse this consent.[14]

Two points have to be noted here: St John uses the word "knowingly", because a person can fall into imperfections without having knowledge or control in the matter. Secondly, it is a question of *habitual* appetites, "because certain scattered acts of different desires are not such a hindrance to union".

Mediocrity in the spiritual life becomes evident in the attitude of mind that remains content with habitual imperfections, on the grounds that they are only imperfections. Because they are habitual, these imperfections catch up on us later in life and cause us much more suffering than that which we had first wanted to avoid. Since these imperfections are in fact a voluntary departure from what God wants, we are moving out of his plan of love for us. The departure may be very slight at first, but habitual appetites grow with our growth and our departure from God's plan might be considerable in the end. A young tree can be easily rooted up, not so when it has become a large oak. It should not surprise us, then, when St John gives some examples of habitual imperfections that seem to be quite trivial:

the common habit of loquacity; a small attachment one never really desires to conquer, for example, to a person, to clothing, to a book or a cell, or to the way food is prepared, and to other trifling conversations and little satisfactions in tasting, knowing, and hearing things, etc.[15]

Even though the imperfection may be very small, as long as the attachment continues the person is like a bird tied by no more than a thin thread; it is impossible to make progress in perfection or reach the freedom of divine union. Failure to break the thin thread of attachment is "a matter for deep sorrow". St John is thinking of the long-term effect of not breaking with some "childish thing which God has requested them to conquer for love of Him".

> We have witnessed many persons, whom God favored with progress in detachment and freedom, fall from happiness in their spiritual exercises and end up by losing everything merely because they began to indulge in some slight attachment to conversation and friendship under the color of good. For by this attachment they gradually emptied themselves of both holy solitude and the spirit and joy of God. All this happened because they did not put a stop to their initial satisfaction and sensitive pleasure and preserve themselves for God in solitude.[16]

From what St John has written he believes it will be clear why the name "night" can appropriately be given to this inner detachment from all created things, and why it is necessary to practise detachment if we are to learn how to turn our love wholly towards God, so that created things will be loved not for our own selfish ends but in him and for him. It remains to provide a method, a set of practical guidelines, for entering the active night. This method is the subject of chapter thirteen.

THE GUIDELINES OF CHAPTER THIRTEEN

The chapter opens with a distinction between the *manner* and the *method* of entering the night of sense. In the *Ascent*, the manner is active. In the *Dark Night* the manner is passive. "In the passive way an individual does nothing, for God accomplishes the work in him, while he acts as the recipient." The aim of this chapter thirteen of I *Ascent* is therefore to prescribe a method for the *active* manner of entering the night. This is done under four headings:

1 the five external senses;
2 the four passions of joy, hope, fear, and grief;
3 the threefold concupiscence;
4 counsels for reaching the summit.

St John rightly calls it "an abridged method". The various counsels are not elaborated, nor are explanations given, since the previous chapters had already done the ground work. There are, however, certain cautions or qualifying statements which the beginner would do well to note before taking up the practice of what appears in the written word. The method on the whole is easy to understand, but the practical application of the counsels requires a careful examination of the text. St John had no doubt about their validity.

> Though these counsels for conquering the appetites are brief and few in number, I believe they are as profitable and efficacious as they are concise. He who sincerely wants to practice them will need no others, since all the others are included in these.[17]

The construction of the whole method makes it clear that the mind is not to be focused on self-perfection, but is to be centred entirely on Christ. "*First*, have a habitual desire to imitate Christ in all your deeds by bringing your life into conformity with His. You must then study His life in order to know how to imitate Him and behave in all events as He would." This first norm is applied explicitly only to the counsels under the heading of the five senses. But it clearly applies to all the counsels. It is placed "first", all the others are "second".

1 *The five senses*. "If you are offered the satisfaction of hearing (seeing, tasting, etc.) things that have no relation to the service and glory of God, do not desire this pleasure or the hearing

(seeing, tasting, etc.) of these things." Because Christ had no other pleasure, nor desired any, than his Father's will, the disciple who wants to imitate him, must "renounce and remain empty of any sensory satisfaction that is not purely for the honor and glory of God". From a careless reading of this text we might think that St John rules out all sense satisfaction. Yet the honour and glory of God is served by many of our legitimate sense pleasures: for example, when we enjoy art or recreation, or a meal in company with friends. Not all of them, however, are "purely" for the glory of God. Other motives may be present more or less. We might wonder why there must be only one motive, why not other motives along with the principal one? We find the answer in Christ, who always had only the one motive. Moreover, in a former chapter (5), St John had explained: "He who loves something together with God undoubtedly makes little of God, for he weighs in the balance with God an object far distant from God." We should not love something with God which we do not love purely for God. To love God, and all else in and for God, integrates our lives in a single objective and gives us a strong sense of purpose.

It is not a matter of rejecting sense pleasure in general, still less of developing an unhealthy attitude towards it. St John may have had this kind of objection in mind when he added a most important qualification on renouncing the gratification of the senses: "*Do this out of love for Jesus Christ*". If we examine our lives in the light of St John's teaching, and perhaps with the help of wise friends, we shall probably identify some things that are good in themselves but to which we are excessively attached. When it is done out of love, the effort to become detached is not experienced as deprivation, and it brings its own healing with it. A greater and better love will not hesitate "to leave the senses as though in darkness, mortified, and empty of pleasure. With such vigilance you will gain a great deal in a short time".

2 *The four passions* are treated here insofar as their object is some sense gratification. Afterwards, in III *Ascent*, they are dealt with in connection with the purification of the will, so that "from a human and lowly will it may be changed into the divine will, made identical with the will of God".[18] Here St John gives "a complete remedy" for the mortification of the four natural passions. These can be like storms on the calm sea of the soul, depriving it of the peace of the Holy Spirit. The prescribed remedy is:

> Endeavour to be inclined always
>> not to the easiest, but to the most difficult;
>> not to the most delightful, but to the harshest;
>> not to the most gratifying, but to the less pleasant;
>> not to what means rest for you, but to hard work;
>> not to the consoling, but to the unconsoling;
>> not to the most, but to the least; . . .

It should be noted that St John is not telling us here always to choose the hardest, the most difficult, the lowest, etc. There may be times when that should be done, but the advice here is not concerned with absolute choice. It says: *endeavour to be inclined always* so to choose. The purpose is tranquillity in the passions, which is fostered by this attitude of mind or readiness of will contrary to what our natural passions may thirst for. Basically, it is an openness of heart for God's will. St John knows that it is not "natural" to embrace these practices. His advice is gentle: *try to* overcome the repugnance of your will towards them. Even though St John is leading the soul to the highest perfection, he did not say: always choose the hardest, the most difficult, etc. He knew we might not have the strength to benefit from that kind of choice. We are not to attempt something beyond our reach before we are spiritually prepared for it, even though it may in itself be the best thing to do. So He adds: "If you sincerely put them into practice *with order and discretion*, you will discover in them great delight and consolation."

3 *The threefold concupiscence.* Our natural tendencies need to be controlled or "mortified" because we begin in a state of disorientation. At the root of the disorder is what is traditionally called the threefold concupiscence, enumerated by St John Evangelist: "If anyone loves the world, love for the Father is not in him. For all that is in the world, the lust of the flesh and the lust of the eyes and the pride of life, is not of the Father but is of the world" (1 John 2: 16). St John of the Cross is following the traditional doctrine as he probably read it in the *Summa* of St Thomas Aquinas. The threefold concupiscence is there spoken of as the cause of sin (I II q77 a5). In the previous article, it is stated that self-love is the cause of every sin, and also that "concupiscence, whereby a man desires good for himself, is reduced to self-love as to its cause" (art. 4 ad 2).[19] We are left then with one single root of disorder, namely, self-love. It is this that St John of the Cross attacks in the set of rules of this section. It is well to have in mind also what St Thomas wrote about self-love: "Well-ordered self-love, whereby man desires a fitting good for himself is right and natural; but it is inordinate self-love, leading to contempt of God, that Augustine reckons to be the cause of sin".[20] St John of the Cross simply takes this inordinate self-love as a target, showing how it should be dealt with in thought, word, and deed.

> *First*, try to *act* with contempt for yourself and desire that all others do likewise.
> *Second*, endeavor to *speak* in contempt of yourself and desire all others to do so.
> *Third*, try to *think* lowly and contemptuously of yourself and desire that all others do the same.

Any abridged method is open to misinterpretation. If these

counsels were taken to mean a continual self-depreciation they could be harmful, especially if the door of a divine confidence were not opened. The disorder St John has in mind is selfishness in our actions, self-centred thoughts, and a use of speech that takes little account of the common good. He does not think we shall succeed in overcoming these defects completely. He says: try to act, endeavour to speak, try to think in contempt of self. Since disordered self-love is a root-obstacle to union with God, it can be cured in no other way than by entering the night.

4 *Counsels for reaching the summit* are repeated from St John's sketch of the *Mount* at the beginning of the book (*K.*, pp. 66, 67). They have a more absolute character because they were addressed primarily to persons more advanced on the spiritual journey. The whole "abridged method" is not for beginners only. Self-denial remains a constant. Ascetical principles are not something that can be left aside as we advance. The same principles remain but their application varies with the different stages. Everything has to be done with "order and discretion". The same set of instructions is interpreted and applied in a different manner to different situations. The following counsels appropriate for the spiritual night are applied here to the active night of sense:

> To reach satisfaction in all
>   desire its possession in nothing.
> To come to possess all
>   desire the possession of nothing.
> To arrive at being all
>   desire to be nothing.
> To come to the knowledge of all
>   desire the knowledge of nothing.
> To come to the pleasure you have not
>   you must go by a way in which you enjoy not.

> To come to the knowledge you have not
>   you must go by a way in which you know not . . .

The absolute character of this self-denial is balanced by the absolute treasure which motivates it. The soul is taken beyond all things only in order to reach him who is beyond all things. Even if, at the summit, absolutely everything has to be sacrificed, this is for the possession of the All.

> And when you come to the possession of the all
>   you must possess it without wanting anything.
> Because if you desire to have something in all
>   your treasure in God is not purely your all.[21]

In presenting this "abridged method", St John was not unmindful of the power of human passions and appetites. Reason should be in control, but frequently we find that appetite has its own way. In our fallen state, nature does not provide a remedy. A greater and better love, a stronger and more powerful desire, has to enter the contest.

> For the sensory appetites are moved and attracted toward sensory objects with such cravings that if the spiritual part of the soul is not fired with other more urgent longings for spiritual things, the soul will neither be able to overcome the yoke of nature nor enter the night of sense; nor will it have the courage to live in the darkness of all things by denying its appetites for them.[22]

Theoretically, the love of God should be more than enough to conquer all the cravings of appetite. St John sees that the ordinary "love of one's Spouse" will not measure up to what is required. It must be "an enkindling with longings of love". The enkindling takes place in the dark night. So the soul goes out, "Fired with love's urgent longings". Just as the passions seem to have an ingenuity of their own in leading reason astray, so these longings of love have their own cleverness and diligence. They sweeten and ease all the hardships of the night of sense, even making its trials and dangers a matter for delight. St John does not elaborate here on this aspect of the night: "It is better to experience all of this and meditate upon it than to write of it".[23]

The passions and appetites were meant by God to be good servants in the house of the soul. Their tendency since original sin is to become masters. By the "sheer grace" of a fervent love, the house of the soul is set in order again, the desires are lulled to sleep, the soul goes out to its Beloved in the night, unseen. The "wretched state of captivity" is ended.

St John sums up his teaching in a final conclusion:

Until slumber comes to the appetites through the mortification of sensuality, and until this very sensuality is stilled in such a way that the appetites do not war against the spirit, the soul will not walk out to genuine freedom, to the enjoyment of union with the Beloved.[24]

NOTES

1   I *A.*, Prol. 1, *K.*, p. 69
2   I *A.*, Prol. 3, *K.*, p. 70
3   I *A.*, Prol. 3, *K.*, p. 70
4   I *A.*, Prol. 7, *K.*, p. 72
5   III *A.*, 44/4, *K.*, p. 289
6   I *A.*, 3/4, *K.*, p. 77
7   I *A.*, 4/6, *K.*, p. 80
8   I *A.*, 5/4, *K.*, p. 82
9   I *A.*, 5/7, *K.*, p. 83
10 I *A.*, 8/4, *K.*, p. 90
11 I *A.*, 10/4, *K.*, p. 95
12 I *A.*, 11/1, *K.*, p. 96

13   I *A.*, 11/2, *K.*, p. 96
14   I *A.*, 11/3, *K.*, p. 96
15   I *A.*, 11/4, *K.*, p. 97
16   I *A.*, 11/5, *K.*, p. 98
17   I *A.*, 13/2, *K.*, p. 102
18   III *A.*, 16/3, *K.*, p. 238
19   *Summa Theologica*, translated by the Fathers of the English Dominican Province, Maryland, Christian Classics, 1981, vol. II, p. 937
20   I II q 77 a 4 ad 1, *ibid.*
21   I *A.*, 13/10, 11, *K.*, p. 103, 104
22   I *A.*, 14/2, *K.*, p. 105
23   I *A.*, 14/3, *K.*, p. 105
24   I *A.*, 15/2, *K.*, p. 106

9

THE ACTIVE
NIGHT OF SPIRIT

I: JOURNEY IN FAITH

From St Augustine onwards, Christian writers in the West thought of the soul as having three capacities or powers: the intellect, the faculty by which it could know and understand; the memory, which stores its knowledge and life experiences; and the will, the power to desire, choose, and enjoy. St John saw that these three faculties could be paired with the three "theological virtues", faith, hope, and love (1 Corinthians 13:13), which differ from natural virtues in that they are infused gifts. The intellect can approach God through faith, the memory through hope, the will through love. In II *Ascent*, St John treats of the purifying effect of faith on the intellect. In III *Ascent* he deals with the memory and the will insofar as they are purified by hope and charity. The exercise of these theological virtues is the special task of the soul during the active night of the spirit. These virtues divinize our natural activity of thinking and loving, so that we can embrace God himself in love. Theological virtue is our active way of opening the door to divine intimacy. In fact, the door had to be opened for us by God in Christ, who was sent to us for this very purpose. We are free to retain only our human way of knowing and loving, or we can opt for this new power of acting in a divine way.

The classic text for a doctrine of faith is chapter eleven of the

THE JOURNEY IN FAITH

ASCENT BOOK II   Intellect — Faith

	Chapters
The nature of union with God	5
The extent of self-denial required	7
The proximate means for intellect	1–9
Division of intellect — knowledge	10

Christ the Model
Faith

Knowledge

natural
- through external bodily senses (*Book I*)
- through reflection (meditation) — 12–15

(The 3 signs 13–14)

supernatural
(transcending natural ability and capacity)

Christ the only Word

corporal
- exterior senses
- interior senses (imagination)
  - visions
  - revelations
  - locutions
  - feelings — 16–21

spiritual
- distinct and particular
  - visions
  - revelations
  - locutions
  - spiritual feelings — 23–32
- vague, dark, general (imparted in faith)
  - **Contemplation**

Letter to the Hebrews where it says that "faith is the substance of things to be hoped for" (*Confraternity* translation) or "faith is the assurance of things hoped for, the conviction of things not seen" (RSV). Originally the Letter to the Hebrews was sent to persecuted Christians, assuring them that their sufferings had a divine meaning. Their faith was a guarantee of the unseen realities for which they hoped. They were even told that the heavenly homeland to which they looked forward was in some way already present. They were even now living that wonderful reality and their sufferings would soon end in glory.

Some scripture commentators say that the meaning of the word "substance" in the Greek world at that time was something like title deeds of property, the whole body of documents bearing on ownership. For example, if a father gave his son the title deeds of some property which he could not actually enjoy until he had come of age, the son could say that he possessed the property. He had it in substance. St Thomas Aquinas, commenting on this text of Hebrews, said that it was not strictly a definition of faith, though it contained all the elements of a definition. He went on to explain: we are accustomed to use the name "substance" for the first beginning of a thing, especially when the whole subsequent thing is contained in that first beginning. So faith is said to be the substance of things hoped for because the first beginning of those things is already brought about by the assent of faith. So if we wanted a strict definition of faith, St Thomas would put it this way: faith is a habit of the mind by which eternal life is already begun in us, making our intellect assent to what we do not see.[1]

St John of the Cross follows this line of thought. He gives a very thorough doctrine on faith, preferring it to heavenly favours like visions or revelations. "In a way, this dark, loving knowledge, which is faith, serves as a means for the divine union in this life as does the light of glory for the clear vision of God in the next."[2]

His mind focused particularly on the content of faith, "the glory and the light of the divinity". Despite his reputation for a "dark night" theology, his treatise on faith is a doctrine of divine light. Faith, he says, is like the cloud for the Chosen People which, though dark in itself, could illumine the night:

> How wonderful it was – a cloud, dark in itself, could illumine the night! This was related to illustrate how faith, a dark and obscure cloud to man (also a night in that it blinds and deprives him of his natural light), illumines and pours light into the darkness of his soul by means of its own darkness.[3]

We are confronted here with authentic light, superior to flashes of genius or other kinds of spiritual enlightenment. St John praises the dark night as being "more lovely than the dawn". In the liturgical hymn of the Easter Vigil, the loveliness of "this blessed night" comes from the fact that the Light of Christ has overcome the darkness. So St John was attracted to faith because it has its focal point in Christ, the Splendour of the Father. In a brief commentary on Psalm 18:3, "Day unto day takes up the story and night unto night makes known the message", he says:

> Expressed more clearly, this means: The day, which is God (in bliss where it is day), communicates and pronounces the Word, His Son, to the angels and blessed souls, who are now day; and this He does that they may have knowledge and enjoyment of Him. And the night, which is faith present in the Church Militant, where it is still night, manifests knowledge to the Church and, consequently, to every soul. This knowledge is night to a man because he does not yet possess the clear, beatific wisdom, and because faith blinds him as to his own natural light.[4]

The parallelism of the psalm brings out how the Word spoken in "day" to the blessed (causing their blessedness) is the same

Word spoken now in "night" to us as we make our journey in faith to eternal light.

The second book of the *Ascent*, which St John says is "most important for persons of genuine spirituality", shows how the intellect of the contemplative is purified by faith so that it can be united with God. The whole book (II *Ascent*) is a treatise on faith, bringing us new insights into its nature and function in the active night of spirit. The nature of faith is made clear by the famous illustration from the scripture account of the soldiers of Gideon.

> According to the account, all the soldiers held lamps in their hands, yet did not see the light because the lamps were hidden in darkness within earthenware jars. But when these jars were broken, the soldiers immediately beheld the shining light. (Judges 7:16–20) Faith, typified by those clay jars, contains the divine light. When faith has reached its end and is shattered by the ending and breaking of this mortal life, the glory and light of the divinity, the content of faith, will at once begin to shine.[5]

These words, describing the content of faith, are crucial for an understanding of St John's teaching and for an appreciation of the function of faith in II *Ascent*, where obscure contemplation is preferred to all forms of particular knowledge, earthly or heavenly. It is true that God's gifts of visions, revelations, and spiritual feelings raise the soul to a high level of contemplation and love of God. The remembrance of these gifts also produces beneficial effects. Nevertheless, pure faith, and freedom from reliance on these gifts, "elevate it (the soul) much more, and without its knowing how or whence this elevation comes".[6] For faith is a divine light and it is rooted more firmly in the soul by means of darkness and spiritual poverty. Since it exceeds the capacity of the intellect, it has to be received in darkness. But even as darkness, it raises the intellect to a divine level, the level at which union with God can take place. For St John, faith is the only proximate and proportionate means to union with God. "The more intense a man's faith, the closer is his union with God."

The divine light, because of its excessive brightness, oppresses and disables an understanding not yet prepared to receive it. Hence there may be crises of faith, temptations against faith, trial of faith, night of faith. A simple crisis of faith sometimes occurs when God's commandments become burdensome and an escape into intellectual difficulties about the faith seems to be a respectable way out. In other cases of genuine striving for a full Christian life, temptations against the faith are common. For example, the human supports of our faith are taken for granted: our parents, Christian environment, books, music, liturgy, devout friends. In order to strengthen our faith, God may remove some of these props. The result might be a severe test for the soul. The classic example of a trial of faith is the case of Abraham, who had it on God's word that through his son Isaac he would have a long posterity. Afterwards he was told to sacrifice this son of promise. The command and the promise did not tally. No human reckoning could have solved the difficulty. Abraham believed that there must be a divine solution which transcended his own way of thinking. His faith was credited to him as justice. The night of faith occurs after a person has come successfully through trial and temptation. God rewards this faith by deepening his own companionship with the soul. The darkness then gradually thickens and the former human supports are removed. Pure faith alone remains. Since the soul at this point loves God intensely and desires only him, this darkness, "a wall reaching up to heaven", shutting out all apparent communication, is a very severe trial. The very perfection of the divine light oppresses the intellect and there is no other source left to build up the soul's confidence. Its guarantee and certitude have to come out of the darkness. The dark cloud of faith will illumine the night. The way of faith may puzzle us when we cannot have explanations for what is required of us. We may feel frustrated for lack of a clear objective. The darkness of faith involves a profound spiritual self-denial. St John compares it to a complete, temporal, natural, and spiritual death. "This is a venture in which God alone is sought and gained, thus only God ought to be sought and gained".[7]

A summary of this theme and of the whole book (II *Ascent*) may be found in chapter four. It brings out clearly what most people discover for themselves: there cannot be any clear path to a hidden God. Just when we think we understand, our grasp of the way escapes us. The most that can be attained is the obscure encounter with God which faith alone provides. It is this obscure encounter with God that St John had in mind when he said that faith is the only proximate and proportionate means to union with God. To advance towards God, then, a person must be content with the obscurity of an unknown way, taking faith for guide.

> Like a blind man he must lean on dark faith, accept it for his guide and light, and rest on nothing of what he understands, tastes, feels, or imagines. All these perceptions are a darkness that will lead him astray. Faith lies beyond all this understanding, taste, feeling, and imagining.[8]

In these chapters on the obscurity of faith St John reminds us that he is now addressing the "intellect of the spiritual man, particularly of him whom God has favoured with the state of contemplation".[9] This includes all those who for one reason or another, through visions or revelations, or other spiritual experiences, might be tempted to think that they now know the ways of God. They may even have good reason for thinking so, like Abraham who had God's word for it. It is then that the apparent contradictions become baffling and humiliating. In chapter four, St John points out the darkness of soul required for effective guidance through faith to supreme contemplation:[10]

> As regards this road to union, entering on the road means leaving one's own road, or better, moving on to the goal; and turning from one's own mode implies entry into what has no mode, that is, God. A person who reaches this state no longer has any modes or methods, still less is he – nor can he be – attached to them. I am referring to modes of understanding, taste, and feeling. Within himself, though, he possesses all methods, like one who though having nothing yet possesses all things. (2 Corinthians 6:10) By being courageous enough to pass beyond the interior and exterior limits of his nature, he enters within supernatural bounds – bounds that have no mode, yet in substance possess all modes.[11]

The way of darkness is specifically the contemplative way. It is the journey in faith. St John is careful not to suggest this way for beginners. The beginner, unable to be occupied in this obscure, general, loving knowledge which is communicated through faith, must employ the remote means which is meditation. He or she must reflect upon particular ideas and images for the purpose of acquiring some knowledge and love of God.[12] In the initial stage the soul is still attached to sense experience and needs this support in order to advance. God respects this weakness. By means of the senses he draws beginners to himself. But when they have passed beyond that stage to the beginnings of contemplation, St John advises them to turn away during prayer-time from all particular knowledge, that is, from whatever can be picked up by the active intellect. They must turn away from anything that could be described as distinct, particular knowledge, and engage in a general loving attentiveness to God through faith. For it is through faith that contemplation is infused.

The Holy Spirit enlightens the intellect according to the mode of its recollection. Since there is no better recollection than faith, the Holy Spirit will not enlighten the soul in any other recollection more than in faith.[13] Thus St John's whole argument is based on the principle that faith is the highest form of enlightenment, transcending all human understanding, taste and feeling, even that which is divinely communicated. Therefore the soul must not rest on what it understands, tastes, feels, or imagines. For if it does not blind itself to those lesser lights and remain in darkness, it will not reach that which is so much greater.

St John guides the soul in faith through all forms of knowledge, including visions, revelations, and spiritual feelings, to the freedom of an obscure, general, loving awareness of God.[14] Through its own efforts the soul must empty itself of attachment to any kind of particular knowledge, no matter how high or supernatural it may be. The language used for this active role sounds negative and the experience seems to be that of despoliation. But the option is for something infinitely greater. Every option implies a negation of alternatives, and the alternatives in this case would hinder the attainment of a supreme good. In St John's doctrine, the content of faith is the supreme good, and the soul's freedom is exercised in preferring this to highly attractive spiritual alternatives. This is the contemplative preference for the darkness, out of love for the brightness that lies hidden there. "Its clarity is never darkened, / And I knew that every light has come from it / Although it is night."[15] Alternatives to this good might be, for example, the particular insights by which the Holy Spirit enlightens the mind. It is not so obvious why the soul should deprive itself of these. But the choice is between particular truths and all God's wisdom communicated in faith.

Freedom To Rejoice

In that illumination of truths the Holy Spirit indeed communicates some light to the soul, yet the light given in faith – in which there is no clear understanding – is qualitatively as different from the other as is the purest gold from the basest metal, and quantitatively as the sea from a drop of water. In the first kind of illumination, wisdom concerning one, two, or three truths, etc., is communicated; in the second, all God's wisdom is communicated in general, that is, the Son of God, Who is imparted to the soul in faith.[16]

In all his teaching on faith, St John endeavours to free the soul from the tangible, particular good, however spiritual it may be, so that the person might learn to abide in the pure and simple light of God, and be perfectly transformed into it. If, on the contrary, one preferred the immediate and more attractive light, "he would hinder the general, limpid, and simple light of the spirit".[17] The interference of "his cloudy thoughts" would be an obstacle to the light of God. The function of faith, therefore, is to eliminate the impediments and veils, figures, forms, and images – the wrappings of spiritual communications[18] – and to opt for what is essentially given in the darkness. The soul "in its simplicity and purity will then be immediately transformed into the simple and pure Wisdom, the Son of God".[19]

NOTES

1 *Summa Theologica*, translated by the Fathers of the English Dominican Province, Maryland, Christian Classics, 1981, II II q 4 a 1
2 II *A.*, 24/4, *K.*, p. 190
3 II *A.*, 3/5, *K.*, p. 111
4 II *A.*, 3/5, *K.*, p. 111
5 II *A.*, 9/3, *K.*, p. 130
6 II *A.*, 24/8, *K.*, p. 192

7 II *A.*, 7/3, *K.*, p. 122
8 II *A.*, 4/2, *K.*, p. 113
9 II *A.*, 7/13, *K.*, p. 125
10 Title of chapter four, *K.*, p. 112
11 II *A.*, 4/5, *K.*, p. 114
12 II *A.*, 14/2, *K.*, p. 142
13 II *A.*, 29/6, *K.*, p. 205
14 This is the theme of II *Ascent* from chapter sixteen to the end
15 *Song of the soul that rejoices in knowing God through faith*, stanza 5, *K.*, p. 723
16 II *A.*, 29/6, *K.*, p. 205
17 II *A.*, 15/3, *K.*, p. 149
18 II *A.*, 16/11, *K.*, p. 153
19 II *A.*, 15/4, *K.*, p. 149

10

THE ACTIVE
NIGHT OF SPIRIT

II: CONSECRATION OF MEMORY

The first fifteen chapters of III *Ascent* are a treatise on the role of
memory in the contemplative life. Since the contemplative life is
a life of love, memory has its importance. For when people love
each other, to forget is unthinkable. Hence the contemplative life
is an abiding remembrance of God. It is clear in these chapters
that St John is not writing only about time set aside for prayer,
but also about an attitude that runs profoundly through the
whole of life.

The term "memory" needs to be given a somewhat wider
interpretation than we are normally used to giving it, if we are to
understand St John's meaning. For him, as for us, memory is the
soul's capacity to store and recall a person's knowledge and
life-experience. A life-experience is seldom a once-for-all event.
Whether pleasant or painful, we have a tendency to live our
experiences over and over again. It is memory that enables us to
do this. When we recall time and place in detail, locating the past
as past, we are using sense memory. Not all of our memories are
so tied to the particulars of sense life. We have habitual
knowledge in our intellect which can be recalled. This intellectual recall is also memory. As a faculty it is spiritual and it is
the memory St John is dealing with in the active night of spirit. It
is purified by the theological virtue of hope just as the intellect is

THE CONSECRATION OF MEMORY

ASCENT BOOK III
III A. chapters 1–15

Memory (Hope)

Objects of knowledge in the memory (1)	Harm from acceptance	Benefits from rejection	
natural (2) — hearing, sight, smell, taste, touch	things of the world (3) — falsehood, imperfections, appetites, judgements, waste of time	(6)	Detachment
	the devil (4)		
	hinders moral good (5) and deprives of spiritual good		
supernatural (imaginative) (7) — visions, revelations, locutions, feelings	deception (8) presumption (9) devil's interference (10) hinders union (11) low estimate of God (12)	(13)	Poverty of spirit
spiritual (14)			

HOPE { Detachment, Poverty of spirit }

Summary (15)

purified by faith. Like the intellect, it deals with knowledge that comes through the senses and through the imagination, as well as with habitual knowledge stored in the intellect. So it has a large field of action. St John divides the objects of memory into natural, imaginative, and spiritual, though he deals only with the first two of these. The treatment of "spiritual reminiscence" was already sufficiently presented when dealing with the purification of the intellect in II *Ascent*. St John did not mean thereby to reduce the scope of memory or lessen the importance of its function in the conduct of the spiritual life. This may be illustrated by a text from St Bonaventure (AD 1217–1274) which shows how, within the Augustinian system which St John follows in his division of faculties, memory could be conceived as having a very wide existential function and as being oriented to the future:

> The function of memory is to retain and represent not only present, corporeal and temporal things but also successive, simple and eternal things. For the memory retains the past by remembrance, the present by reception and the future by foresight ... the memory is an image of eternity, whose indivisible presence extends to all times.[1]

In III *Ascent* St John is dealing with the active purification of the memory in all these aspects. He is addressing particularly those advancing in contemplation so that they may consecrate their memory to God and so be united with him in the memory. His instructions are for a positive reorientation of the memory towards God, away from what we can imagine and away from clinging to past experience.

Hope is a theological virtue, a gift from God, drawing the soul towards an infinite, personal Good made known by faith. It is the stirring of desire for that Good. It orientates the mind and does not allow it to wander away from its object. Hope consecrates the memory by keeping it free for God. "To him who longs for something great, all lesser things seem small."[2] Hope leaves the memory dispossessed and empty for the one great thing the contemplative really wants.

By its action on the imaginative aspect of the memory, hope perfects the memory so that it will not delay the soul on its journey to God by attachment to creatures. By reorienting the trust and confidence of the soul towards God it prevents the soul from relying on itself, or on any special favour it has received from God, or on the kind of life it leads, as the ground of its confidence for the receiving of eternal life. Its confidence must be in God alone, in perfect poverty of spirit and childlike trust. The soul must be drawn away from its natural supports and raised above all distinct knowledge to supreme hope in the incomprehensible God.

St John's treatise on memory is straightforward and easy to read, provided we keep in mind his mode of procedure. He begins by describing the state of perfect union, when the memory is taken up completely with God. From that he draws conclusions for proficients, whom he is guiding in these chapters, for it is they who have the task of actively purifying the memory. He adds something for beginners, describing a number of natural benefits that result from control of the memory. The treatise does not have to establish theological principles, for these have already been dealt with in the account of the purification of the intellect by faith.

We have already given instructions for the intellect, the first faculty of the soul, so that in all its apprehensions it may be united with God through pure faith, the first theological virtue. The same has to be done for the other two faculties, memory and will. . . . it is unnecessary to enlarge so much in our treatise on these faculties, since in the instructions given for the intellect (the receptacle in its own way of all the other objects) we have covered a great portion of the matter.[3]

In each case it is a matter of the faculty being detached (emptied, purified) from all that it relies on in a purely human fashion, to be filled instead by God.

Like St Teresa (*Mansions* V), St John makes a distinction between the passing grace of union, and the established state of union, which is the end towards which the soul is being guided. He describes the effect of the passing grace on the memory: "That divine union empties and sweeps the phantasy of all forms and knowledge, and elevates the memory to the supernatural".[4] It may produce great forgetfulness in the memory. The soul's clinging to any kind of "apprehensible knowledge" would be a lack of openness to the reception of this grace. From this we learn what kind of active preparation is needed that God may produce these touches of union.

> As often as distinct ideas, forms, and images occur to him, he should immediately, without resting in them, turn to God with loving affection, in emptiness of everything rememberable. He should not think or look upon these things for a longer time than is sufficient for the understanding and fulfilment of his obligations, if they refer to this. And then he should consider these ideas without becoming attached or seeking gratification in them, lest they leave their effects in the soul. Thus a man is not required to cease recalling and thinking about what he must do and know, for, since he is not attached to the possession of these thoughts, he will not be harmed.[5]

St John is referring not only to memories that seem to have no usefulness – unnecessary luggage on our journey to God – but to all particular or distinct ideas, the remembrance of all things that are not God. But he reminds us that this instruction is for those

advancing in contemplation to union with God, not for beginners, "who have to prepare themselves through these discursive
apprehensions".[6] The instruction also has certain qualifications.
Thus a person is to remember whatever is necessary for the
performance of their duties. Visible images of God and the saints
are not to be done away with (St John is writing at the height of
the Reformation) but "we are explaining the difference between
these images and God, and how souls should use the painted
image in such a way that they do not suffer an impediment in
their movement towards the living image".[7] In this positive
movement towards God, the person may and should remember
the spiritual knowledge of God that he himself imparts, beyond
words and images, and "the effect of light, love, delight, and
spiritual renewal" that these touches of his love produce in the
soul.

Just as we have to put a cloud of unknowing between ourselves
and God as regards the intellect, so also we have to put a cloud of
forgetting between ourselves and creatures as regards the
memory. The principle St John lays down is the annihilation of
the memory with regard to all particular knowledge as an
absolute requirement for perfect union with God. The memory
cannot at the same time be united with God and with the forms
of distinct knowledge, since God has no form or image that the
memory could comprehend. St John points to the experience of
union. When the memory is perfectly united to God it retains no
form or figure. At this stage it may be in great forgetfulness,
without remembrance of anything. It is absorbed in the supreme
Good and, being thus completely taken up with God, it cannot
remember anything else. Because of these touches of union in
the memory, the soul remains at times in such great forgetfulness
that it must "occasionally force itself and struggle in order to
remember something".[8] These suspensions of the memory are
more frequent at the beginning. Later on when the soul has

reached perfection, it will not need to force or struggle. Then God remembers for it. As far as the faculty of memory is concerned, union with God does not in the end mean forgetfulness but a state of loving activity in which God's Spirit makes it "know what must be known and ignore what must be ignored, remember what ought to be remembered".[9] All the first stirrings of the faculties in union are under the influence of God. St John gives an example:

> A person will ask a soul in this state for prayers. The soul will not remember to carry out this request through any form or idea of that person remaining in the memory. If it is expedient to pray for him (that is, if God wants to receive prayer for this person), God will move its will and impart a desire to do so; at times God will give it a desire to pray for others whom it has never known or heard of.[10]

Perfect union with God is not usually so continuous that a person's faculties are always moved divinely. But there are some who are very habitually moved by God and not themselves. The works and prayers of these people are always effective. The Blessed Virgin Mary has traditionally been regarded as the supreme example of the contemplative, so St John writes:

> Such was the prayer and work of our Lady, the most glorious Virgin. Raised from the very beginning to this high state, she never had the form of any creature impressed in her soul, nor was she moved by any, for she was always moved by the Holy Spirit.[11]

St John reminds his reader that he has been talking about the state of perfect union, the effect of the passive night. It is not his intention in the present book to discuss further the effects brought about by perfect divine union. He is now talking to people who have to move along by their own activity from the beginnings of contemplation towards the state of perfect union. Obviously this cannot be reached by human effort alone. The individual's preparation has to be proportionate to the gift received. "Thus God will give the habit of perfect divine union when He is pleased to do so and in accordance with the individual's preparation."[12] As regards the preparation of the memory, St John gives his formal advice to the "spiritual" person, the person advancing in contemplation towards union with God:

> Do not store up in the memory the objects of hearing, sight, smell, taste, or touch, but leave them immediately and forget them, and endeavor, if necessary, to be as successful in forgetting them as others are in remembering them. This should be practiced in such a way that no form or figure of any of these objects remains in the memory, as though one were not in the world at all. The memory, as though it were non-existent, should be left free and disencumbered and unattached to any earthly or heavenly consideration.[13]

The "earthly and heavenly" considerations mentioned in the second chapter (III *Ascent*) provide the structure for the chapters that follow. The first section, chapters three to six, shows how hope perfects the memory by detaching it from the imagination of earthly things. The second section, chapters seven to thirteen, deals with hope under the aspect of poverty of spirit, which is detachment even from heavenly things which are not God.

HOPE AND DETACHMENT

St John opens the first section by pointing out how false our mental outlook can become and the number of imperfections we are liable to if we treasure memories that we do not need. These imperfections include waste of time, rash judgements, misrepresentation of our situation, deception from the devil, and unfitting ourselves for the gifts of God. To offset these, he lists the benefits of forgetfulness. *First*, the spiritual person will enjoy peace due to the absence of disturbance that derives from thoughts in the memory. Consequently, the soul will possess purity of conscience, and will be disposed for wisdom. *Second*, the soul is freed from many suggestions and temptations of the devil, because it is on these memories that the devil plays. *Third*, by means of this forgetfulness, the soul is disposed to be moved by the Holy Spirit. But even if no other benefit came to a person through this forgetfulness than freedom from affliction and disturbance, that itself would be an immense advantage and blessing. For the afflictions and disturbances engendered in the soul through adversity are no help to remedy the adversity. Rather, distress and worry ordinarily makes things worse.

> Thus if the whole world were to crumble and come to an end, and all things were to go wrong, it would be useless to get disturbed, for this would do more harm than good. The endurance of all with tranquil and peaceful equanimity not only reaps many blessings, but also helps the soul so that in these very adversities it may succeed in judging them and employing the proper remedy.
> . . . Our nature is so unstable and fragile that even when we disciplined it will hardly fail to stumble upon thoughts with the memory; and these thoughts become a disturbance to a soul that was residing in peace and tranquillity through forgetfulness of all.[14]

The virtue of hope is a remedy for our natural instability. It exerts its sanctifying influence by detaching us from earthly things. Purely earthly considerations give way before the magnetism of eternal life. The supreme Good is preferred as a target for the soul's energies. These energies are thus drawn away from sense pleasure and pride and wealth. Hope, based on a lively faith, shows us that all earthly joys lack both perfection and permanence. It makes us aware that our heart is too great, its aspirations too vast to be satisfied with anything less than God. He is the One who abides. Hope accordingly gives us a high consciousness that all earthly things are on the move towards the fulfilment of an eternal design. We are all pilgrims on the same journey. Hope implies a contemplative awareness of eternal life and a sense of the place eternal values should have in our present existence. Risen with Christ, the true contemplative seeks the things that are above, where Christ is (Colossians 3:1). This goes hand in hand with a profound conviction of the shortness of human life and wisdom of heart to see the vanity of projects that are not related to our true destiny in eternal life.

HOPE AND POVERTY OF SPIRIT

The second section on the purification of the memory treats of hope under the aspect of poverty of spirit. The eternal horizon which draws the soul depends on God's promise. The promise was a revelation of omnipotence and infinite goodness. A person responds to this by complete abandonment and trust in the divine word. Reliance for the fulfilment of the promise must be totally in God himself, not in the remembrance of anything we have received from God, or in anything we ourselves have done. The emptiness of the memory must extend to supernatural and heavenly goods as well as to earthly goods. The soul must not seek anything outside of God as a source of confidence for itself and its destiny. Just as in perfect faith certainty comes out of the darkness, so also in hope the strength of the soul's confidence comes entirely from God. It hopes for him because of himself, that is, because of his trustworthiness and omnipotence. Hope will be more perfect the more it hopes in God alone to the exclusion of all other motives. St John teaches the way that leads to this perfect poverty of spirit, which sets free the movement of hope and disposes the soul for the attainment of the true supernatural good, that is, of God himself. Only the path of nothingness which is perfect detachment and absolute poverty will lead to the All which is God and make certain our possession of him.

In the section on earthly goods, St John had listed the various kinds of harm that come from attachment and the various benefits of detachment. So in this section on heavenly goods, he devotes a chapter each to five kinds of harm that come from remembering the forms and figures of supernatural goods, adding a chapter (13) on the benefits of voiding the memory.

In addition to the tranquillity a person naturally enjoys when freed from images and forms, there is a freedom from care about the discernment of the good ones from the evil, and about how one ought to behave with the different kinds. Finally one would be absolved from the drudgery and waste of time with spiritual directors which would result from desiring the director to discern the good apprehensions from the evil ones and to ascertain the kind of apprehension received. A person does not have to know this, since he should not pay attention to any of these apprehensions.[15]

When the soul pays heed to imaginative apprehensions, it extinguishes the spirit which God infuses by means of them. The teaching therefore is: abandon these apprehensions and behave passively and negatively, because God then moves the soul to what transcends its power and knowledge. A person should pay heed not to the feelings of delight or sweetness, but rather to the feelings of love that are caused by the images. There are some supernatural images which are given precisely so that by being recalled they may produce the effects of love. Then indeed a person may recall them but only for the sake of moving the soul to love.

These are usually so imprinted on it that they last a long time; some are never erased from the soul. These apprehensions produce, almost as often as remembered, divine effects of love, sweetness, light, etc., – sometimes in a greater degree, sometimes in a lesser – because God impressed them for this reason. This is consequently a great grace, for the person upon whom God bestows it possesses within himself a mine of blessings.[16]

The same principle is applied to spiritual knowledge which is without form or image, knowledge of the Creater or of creatures.

But as for knowledge of the Creator, I declare that a person should strive to remember it as often as possible because it will produce in the soul a notable effect. For . . . the communications of this knowledge are touches and spiritual feelings of union with God, the goal to which we are guiding the soul.[17]

Spiritual knowledge of creatures may also be recalled whenever it produces similar good effects, not in order to retain it in the memory but to awaken the knowledge and love of God. But if the remembrance of this knowledge of creatures produces no good effect, the soul should not desire the memory of it.

St John's teaching on memory is based on the word of God, that is, on God's fidelity to his word manifested to us in Christ. The emptiness of the memory is for the sake of the fullness of hope, which consists in the possession and enjoyment of God in eternal life. "For we should hope from Him nothing less than Himself."[18]

NOTES

1 St Bonaventure, *The Soul's Journey into God*, translated by Ewart Cousins, London, SPCK, 1978, Classics of Western Spirituality, p. 80–1, (page 81 begins with the words "image of eternity")
2 St Thomas Aquinas *Summa Theologica*, translated by the Fathers of the English Dominican Province, Maryland, Christian Classics, II II q 17 a 2 ad 3, vol. III, p. 1237
3 III *A.*, 1/1, *K.*, p. 213
4 III *A.*, 2/4, *K.*, p. 215
5 III *A.*, 15/1, *K.*, p. 236
6 III *A.*, 2/1, *K.*, p. 214
7 III *A.*, 15/2, *K.*, p. 236
8 III *A.*, 2/5, *K.*, p. 215
9 III *A.*, 2/9, *K.*, p. 217
10 III *A.*, 2/10, *K.*, p. 217
11 III *A.*, 2/10, *K.*, p. 217
12 III *A.*, 2/13, *K.*, p. 218
13 III *A.*, 2/14, *K.*, p. 218
14 III *A.*, 6/3, *K.*, p. 223, 6/4, *K.*, p. 224
15 III *A.*, 13/1, *K.*, p. 231
16 III *A.*, 13/6, *K.*, p. 233
17 III *A.*, 14/2, *K.*, p. 235
18 St Thomas Aquinas, *Summa Theologica*, II II q 17 a 2

11

THE ACTIVE
NIGHT OF SPIRIT

III: FREEDOM TO REJOICE

The second part of III *Ascent* (chapters 16–45) deals with the active night of the will, that is, the consecration of the will to God through love. When St John teaches that the will must be purified of all its appetites, one might get the impression that for him Christian discipleship means repression of our natural drives and tendencies. Yet the asceticism he teaches is for the sake of freedom. The consecration of the will to God is a release of its full potential. St John therefore opens this treatise with the great precept of Deuteronomy. We are to love God with all our heart, with all our soul, and with all our strength (Deuteronomy 6:5).

This passage contains all that a spiritual man must do and all that I must teach him here if he is to reach God by union of will through charity. In it man receives the command to employ all the faculties, appetites, operations, and emotions of his soul in God so that he may avoid the use of his ability and strength for anything else . . .[1]

Human personality contains a complex of energies, drives and emotions. According to the psychology of St John's time, reaching back to classical times, the human appetite is acted upon by objects in the world of sense (that is, by objects in the

ASCENT BOOK III (cont.)

III A. chapters 16–45   **Will – (Charity)**

Kinds of Goods		Direct joy to God	Harm	Benefit
temporal	– riches, dignities children, relatives, etc.	18	19	20
natural	– beauty, intelligence, talent etc.	21	22	23
sensory	– objects of five senses and imagination	24	25	26
moral	– virtues, mercy, observance of law	27	28	29
supernatural – miracles, prophecy, (benefit others, tongues, healing *gratis datae*)		30	31	32

ACTIVE JOY – VOLUNTARY

(17)

painful {
  distinct
  obscure
} – passive night

spiritual (benefit self)

(33)

delightful {

clear (distinct) (35) {
  motivating
  provocative
  directive
  perfective
}

{
  statues — 36,37
  oratories — 38,39
  recollection — 40
  places of devotion — 41,42
  ceremonies — 43
  Pater Noster — 44
  preaching — 45
}

vague (obscure)
union with God

material world and their forms stored up in the imagination), and by objects of desire in the moral and spiritual realms; but it also has a voluntary part, the rational will, which can actually choose what to love and enjoy. The passions (named from *pati*, to suffer) are the essentially involuntary reactions of the soul to the objects that are presented to it. They induce changes of mood that cloud our judgement, affecting our capacity to estimate the value of things. They tend to be in control, acting against the will. Therefore the task of the ascetical life is to place the will in control over the passions. This active effort prepares the will to receive the divine gift of love, the theological virtue of charity which is friendship with God and love of all else in God and for God.

Since passions and appetites are so often uncontrolled, the word "passion" tended to take on a negative connotation, meaning simply a disordered or inordinate appetite. The Stoics thought in this way, defining passion as *aversa a ratione contra naturam animi commotio* (a disturbance of soul contrary to our reasonable nature), pointing to the idea that passion is in itself a defect. For the Scholastics by contrast, passion is God's good gift. We are responsible for the disorder. Moreover, an object desired by appetite might be good and right in itself but there may be many excellent reasons for not choosing it. When a person is led astray by this kind of good, they acquire what St John calls "a lowly will". So for St John, it is not a question of eliminating the passions, but of ordering them so that all the force of the soul is directed to the love and service of God.

> The entire matter of reaching union with God consists in purging the will of its appetites and feelings, so that from a human and lowly will it may be changed into the divine will, made identical with the will of God.[2]

What needs to be changed or removed is not the appetites themselves but the disorder in their working.

The strength of the soul comprises the faculties, passions, and appetites. All this strength is ruled by the will. When the will directs these faculties, passions, and appetites toward God, turning them away from all that is not God, the soul preserves its strength for God, and comes to love Him with all its might. That a person may effect this, we shall discuss here the purification of the will of all *inordinate* feelings. These inordinate feelings are the sources of unruly appetites, affections, and operations, and the basis for failure to preserve one's strength for God.[3]

When these feelings are unbridled, they are the source of all the vices and imperfections, and when they are in order and composed they give rise to all the virtues.[4]

Following his classical and scholastic predecessors, St John distinguishes four fundamental passions, joy and sorrow, hope and fear.[5] St Thomas Aquinas divides the sensory appetite into two faculties, the "concupiscible" and the "irascible". He assigns three pairs of passions to the concupiscible power: love and hate, desire and aversion, joy and sadness. Similarly there are three groups in the irascible faculty: hope and despair, fear and courage, and anger which has no opposite passion.[6] The first three pairs can be rearranged to form two progressions: love-desire-joy and hatred-aversion-sadness. In other words, love begins when we like something, it turns into wanting and moving towards it, and is fulfilled in joy when we possess the desired object. Joy is the effect and fulfilment of love. If we are able to choose where to direct our love, that is effectively the same as choosing what to enjoy or rejoice in. As St John puts it in this section of the *Ascent*, we can "direct our joy". Similarly, reason and will can order the other passions around this central theme of the love of God.

The passions are natural reactions in the presence of what is agreeable or otherwise. They often anticipate our deliberate choice. But they can be directed. Freedom is our privilege and obligation not to be led astray by our tendencies and desires, but to harness them for a higher good. When we succeed in doing this, we rejoice only in what is purely for God's honour and glory, we hope for nothing else, we are sad about matters that refer to God, and we fear only him. The less strongly the will is fixed on God the more dependent it will be on created things and the more will these four passions reign in it. It will then very easily find joy in what does not deserve rejoicing; it will hope for something that will bring no benefit; it will be sorrowful about something that should rather be a cause for joy; it will fear where there is no cause for fear.

St John does not deal with the whole set of passions as he had promised. Perhaps he felt that enough had been said to guide the reader through to the end. He deals only with the first of the four, namely, joy. Even that is not complete. The subject of joy is systematically presented with numerous divisions. St John probably did not have time to deal with them all. Yet most of the ground is covered and there are many precious counsels to help the reader move along with steady step towards union with God.

Joy is defined by St John as "a satisfaction of the will with esteem for an object it considers fitting. For the will never rejoices unless in something which is valuable and satisfying to it".[7] He divides his treatise on joy according to six kinds of good in which the will may rejoice: temporal, natural, sensory, moral, supernatural, and spiritual. To each of these he devotes three chapters, showing firstly, how we are to direct our joy to God in them; secondly, the harm that will result if we fail to do so; and thirdly the benefits from directing our joy as we ought to. These eighteen chapters cover a vast field of the objects of human striving and rejoicing. Natural goods comprise beauty, elegance, bodily constitution, good intelligence, discretion, and other talents. Sensory goods include whatever can be grasped by the five external senses and the working of the imagination. Supernatural goods are the gifts and graces of God that exceed our natural powers, such as miracles and prophesy. Spiritual goods are "all those that are an aid and motivating force to turning the soul to divine things and to converse with God, as well as a help to God's communication to the soul".[8] Temporal goods include riches, status, dignities as well as children, relatives, and marriages. Of these St John says: "Ink, paper, and time would be exhausted were we to describe the harm which beleaguers the soul because it turns its affections to temporal goods".[9]

However, St John is not a pessimist about our ability for true enjoyment. His whole treatise is an education in joy. The denial he recommends is for the sake of the freedom to rejoice in both earthly and heavenly things. He has much to say even about the temporal advantages of denial and detachment:

> Even if a man does not free his heart of joy in temporal goods for God and for the sake of his obligation to strive after perfection, he ought to do so on account of the resulting temporal advantages, prescinding from the spiritual ones. By dismissing joy over temporal goods . . . he acquires liberty of spirit, clarity of reason, rest, tranquillity, peaceful confidence in God, and, in his will, the true cult and homage of God. He obtains more joy and recreation in creatures through the dispossession of them. He cannot rejoice in them if he beholds them with possessiveness, for this is a care which, like a bond, fastens the spirit to earth and does not allow it freedom of heart.[10]

In the chapters on joy in moral goods, St John raises some interesting questions which he answers with finesse and thoroughness. By moral goods he means:

the virtues and their habits insofar as they are moral; the exercise of any of the virtues; the practice of the works of mercy; the observance of God's law; urbanity and good manners.[11]

Can we rejoice in these moral goods? – For what they are in themselves, moral goods merit rejoicing by their possessor, for they bring with them peace and tranquillity, a right use of reason, and actions resulting from mature deliberation. Humanly speaking, a person cannot have anything better. As Christians, however, we are told to rejoice "in the Lord" (Philippians 4:4). St John seems to be using this principle when he adds that properly speaking we can rejoice in these moral goods only if we see in the light of faith that they are leading us to God. We ought to rejoice in our good works only if we are performing them for the love of God. The value of our good works depends on the love of God practised in them. They are deeper in quality and power the more entire the love of God is found in them and the less self-interest concerning earthly or heavenly joy, comfort or pleasure or praise. St John teaches that we should not set our heart on the pleasure, comfort, or taste that these good works generally entail. We should recollect our joy in God, having only his honour and glory at heart. We should in secret desire only that God be pleased and joyful over them, and have no other personal interest or satisfaction. Thus all the strength of our will in these goods will be recollected in God.

A more common and more interesting question arises in regard to the enjoyment of beautiful scenery or works of art. From his writings and from his life-story we know that St John delighted in the beauty of nature, and he recommended this form of recreation to others. The question here is not about the value of certain kinds of recreation. The point at issue is: when is the contemplation of nature a form of prayer, and when is it merely recreation? As a person of artistic temperament himself, St John gives us a fully-considered reply:

> For when the will in becoming aware of the satisfaction afforded by the object of sight, hearing, or touch, does not stop with this joy but immediately elevates itself to God, rejoicing in Him who motivates and gives strength to its joy, it is doing something very good. The will, then, does not have to avoid such experiences when they produce this devotion and prayer, but it can profit by them, and even ought to for the sake of so holy an exercise. For there are souls who are greatly moved toward God by sensible objects. Yet one should be careful in this matter and take into consideration its effects. Frequently spiritual persons use this refreshment of the senses under the pretext of prayer and devotion to God; and they so perform these exercises that we could call this recreation rather than prayer, and the pleasing of self rather than God. Though the intention of these persons is directed to God, the effect they receive is recreation of the senses, from which they obtain weakness and imperfection more than the quickening of their will and its surrender to God.[12]

St John offers a norm for discerning when the gratification of the senses is beneficial. His test is ultimately liberty of spirit. The person who receives a purely spiritual effect from sensible objects does not have an attachment to them and is none the worse off if they are taken away. The reason is that the true contemplative has a readiness to go to God in and through all things, and

> is so provided for, nourished, and satisfied by God's spirit that it is unwanting and undesirous of anything else ... Yet anyone who does not feel this freedom of spirit in these sensible objects and gratifications, but finds that his will

pauses and feeds upon them, suffers harm from them and ought to turn from their use.[13]

The freedom to rejoice comes from the subjection of sense to reason. Those who do not live according to the senses are free to direct the activity of their faculties to contemplation. The ideal in St John's mind is the state of innocence enjoyed by our first parents. All that they "saw, spoke of, and ate in the garden of paradise served them for more abundant delight in contemplation, since the sensory part of their souls was truly subjected and ordered to reason".[14] When the soul reaches the state of perfect union and transformation in God, it is renewed in this original innocence and purity of heart, and "finds in all things a joyful, pleasant, chaste, pure, spiritual, glad, and loving knowledge of God".[15]

NOTES

1   III *A.*, 16/1, *K.*, p. 237
2   III *A.*, 16/3, *K.*, p. 238
3   III *A.*, 16/2, *K.*, p. 237
4   III *A.*, 16/5, *K.*, p. 238
5   III *A.*, 16/2, *K.*, p. 237
6   *Summa Theologica*, translated by the Fathers of the English Dominican Province, Christian Classics, I II q 23 a 4, vol. II, p. 696
7   III *A.*, 17/1, *K.*, p. 239
8   III *A.*, 33/2, *K.*, p. 273
9   III *A.*, 19/1, *K.*, p. 242
10 III *A.*, 20/2, *K.*, p. 247
11 III *A.*, 27/1, *K.*, p. 260
12 III *A.*, 24/4, *K.*, p. 255
13 III *A.*, 24/6, *K.*, p. 255–6
14 III *A.*, 26/5, *K.*, p. 259
15 III *A.*, 26/6, *K.*, p. 259

12

THE PASSIVE NIGHT OF SENSE

St John of the Cross begins his commentary on the dark night with a prayer:

> May God be pleased to give me His divine light that I may say something worthwhile about this subject, for it is a night so dark and a matter so difficult to treat and expound His enlightenment is very necessary.[1]

Already in the Prologue to the *Ascent*, he had said that the trials and darkness encountered on the way to perfection are so numerous and profound that human science cannot understand them adequately. "He who suffers them will know what the experience is like, but he will find himself unable to describe it." St John himself certainly had a profound experience of the night and no one has so well described it. One thinks especially of his time in the Toledo prison in 1578. It was only in the year following his release that he wrote the poem of the *Dark Night*, a fact which influenced the character of his commentary.

> Before embarking upon an explanation of these stanzas, we should remember that the soul recites them when it has already reached the state of perfection – that is, union with God through love – and has now passed through severe trials and conflicts by means of the spiritual exercise which leads one along the narrow way to eternal life, of which our Saviour speaks in the Gospel. (Matthew 7:13)[2]

DARK NIGHT, BOOK I: The Passive Night of Sense.

The commentary was written between 1582 and 1585, when St John was in Granada. The book immediately became popular, even more so than his other works, so that the *Dark Night* became associated with the name of John of the Cross, as it is today. A modern Carmelite author, Fr Gabriel of St Mary Magdalen, wrote that the doctrine of the *Night* as a means to union of love with God was "perhaps dearer" to St John than all other doctrines. "It constitutes one of his more personal, more appealing, 'discoveries'."[3]

The idea of spiritual darkness was often used by writers before and during St John's lifetime. Francis of Osuna used the metaphor of night but thought of it as punitive rather than as a means to the union of love with God. The name that comes most readily to mind in connection with dark or negative (apophatic) theology is Denys the Areopagite. Hans Urs von Balthasar couples him with St John of the Cross because of their consistent use of this method. His comparison is worth quoting:

> When later on we analyse the Areopagite and John of the Cross – the two theologians who relied most consistently on the apophatic method – we will see that they never divorced it from the cataphatic approach. They could exalt the vertical to such a degree only because they never let go of the horizontal. For this reason they can be considered the two most decidedly aesthetic theologians of Christian history.[4]

Denys (or Dionysius) was a theologian who professed to be Paul's Athenian convert (Acts 17:34) but who in fact wrote, probably in Syria, towards the end of the fifth century AD. He wrote three famous works, *The Celestial Hierarchies*, *The Divine Names* and *Mystical Theology*. In the beginning of his *Mystical Theology* he addresses his reader:

I counsel that, in the earnest exercise of mystic contemplation, you leave the senses and the activities of the intellect and all things that the senses or the intellect can perceive, and all things which are not and things which are, and that you strain upwards in unknowing, to the best of your power, towards union with Him whom neither being nor understanding can contain. For, by the unceasing and absolute renunciation of yourself and all things, you shall in pureness cast all things aside, and be released from all, and so shall be led upwards to the ray of divine darkness which surpasses all being.[5]

Denys enjoyed a great vogue down the centuries, partly because of his supposed discipleship of St Paul and partly because of his mystical terminology which subsequent writers found convenient. How much St John of the Cross was indebted to him is not clear. John of Jesus Mary gave evidence that he saw St John reading Denys, and St John, who seldom quotes authors by name, refers to Denys and to the ray of divine darkness. However, the dark night symbol of obscure contemplation is found even before Denys, in Gregory of Nyssa and Origen. One of its biblical sources is the Song of Songs, St John's favourite book. The frequent references to the psalms in St John's writings seem to indicate that the psalter was never far from his mind and heart. Many so-called "passion psalms" provide the only appropriate language for a person in the depths of the night. "I call for help by day, I cry at night before you. You have laid me in the depths of the tomb, in places that are dark in the depths. Your anger weighs down upon me." (Psalm 87)

As a mystic writing from experience, St John was well aware of how painful the excessive brightness of God can be to the unpurified mind. But his symbol of "night" was used to indicate mystery, rather than only to indicate suffering. What he shows us in the *Dark Night* is that "the thick darkness wherein the soul is enveloped ... hides the precious working whereby the divine mercy completes in it the transformation of love".[6] His poem of the *Dark Night* celebrates the mystery rather than complains of it. The first two stanzas proclaim the effects of the two kinds of purification, of sense and of spirit. The remaining six stanzas rejoice in the marvellous benefits of spiritual illumination and union of love. Even the first two stanzas which speak of purification are really a form of thanksgiving for the "sheer grace" of being able to go out from self "in darkness and security" to the sublime and joyous union with God.[7]

For St John, "Dark Night" was a convenient metaphor for various aspects of the journey to union with God. Just as the human eye, deprived of light, or blinded by excessive brightness, is in darkness, so the other faculties deprived of their proper objects are in a similar position. There may be darkness in the intellect, aridity in the will, affliction in the memory, loneliness or emptiness in the interior senses, deprivation of one kind or another in the exterior senses. All come under the same image of "night". They are all features of a departure from disordered self-love. They cause the soul to die to itself and to all things in order to begin the sweet and delightful life of love. The departure from self takes place in a dark night, but it is a night that guides the soul "more surely than the light of noon".

> O guiding night!
> O night more lovely than the dawn!
> O night that has united
> The Lover with His beloved,
> Transforming the beloved in her Lover.[8]

In the *Ascent of Mount Carmel* the image of night covers the soul's own efforts. In the *Dark Night* it has a new dimension. The dark night "signifies here purgative contemplation, which passively causes in the soul this negation of self and of all things".[9] The mysterious working of God has entered the soul, which is now enfolded in the divine light and love. Infused contemplation has begun its work secretly. The purifying process is gradual, in accordance with human nature. There are two nights or purifications. The first affects the sensitive part of the soul; the second the spiritual part. Both must be purified and "divinized" for union with God.

> This night, which we say is contemplation, causes two kinds of darkness or purgation in spiritual persons according to the two parts of the soul, the sensory and the spiritual. Hence the one night or purgation will be sensory, by which the senses are purged and accommodated to the spirit; and the other night or purgation will be spiritual, by which the spirit is purged and denuded as well as accommodated and prepared for union with God through love.[10]

The first night introduces beginners to the state of contemplation; the second night takes place in those who are already proficients, at the time when God desires to lead them into the state of union. The sensory night is common and happens to many; these are the beginners. The spiritual night is the lot of very few, of those who have been tried and have been prepared for it. The first purgation or night, St John says, is bitter and terrible to the senses. But nothing can be compared to the second, for it is horrible and frightful to the spirit.[11]

SENSE AND SPIRIT

What does St John mean by the sensory and the spiritual parts of the soul? He is talking about two realms of experience rather than two parts of the soul. The soul is a simple, spiritual substance, and has no parts. But it operates both on the level of sense experience and on that of the spirit, and in order to do so it has many different powers. It receives information from the bodily senses, and when it is engaged in a spiritual activity such as meditation it is making use of this stored information through the interior senses of memory and imagination. A philosopher would distinguish this kind of spiritual activity from sense activity, but mystics like St John use a slightly different terminology as a result of their own experience. Sometimes in the experience of union with God, a person may be conscious of very deep peace in their true inner self, and at the same time suffer a tumult of conflicting images, ideas, and reasonings in their superficial self. This experience has led mystics to distinguish two regions of the soul, the realm of sense and the realm of spirit. Sense includes imagination, reasoning, and memory, as these are employed in meditation. Spirit comprises purely intellectual operation, intuition, contemplation, the basic orientation of the will, and love. It is according to this terminology that St John distinguishes the night of sense and the night of spirit.

ACTIVE AND PASSIVE NIGHTS COMPLETE EACH OTHER

The night of sense normally precedes the night of spirit. Both nights have an active and a passive phase. Some writers postulate a preparatory phase to the active night of sense, where the soul retains the initiative, directing its own mortification of desires and appetites. God has not yet intervened. In St John's system, the active and passive nights progress simultaneously. God gradually takes over the direction of the spiritual life. He takes away the initiative of the soul, bringing it into submission to his own direct action. Then the active night and the passive night must complete each other. The first book of the *Ascent* and the first book of the *Dark Night* cover the same ground in its active and passive phases respectively. The passive night, being God's work, is obviously the more important. The soul must respond actively to its demands. Those who have heard a genuine contemplative call will be content with nothing less than an *adequate* response. They will welcome the absolute character of St John's counsels of perfection.

To many persons, these precepts will certainly seem exaggerated: they will see in them an impossible challenge to the moral energies of man. Others, on the contrary, will find them luminous, and their very austerity will seem to them sweet. They will have the impression, on reading Saint Teresa and Saint John of the Cross, that these masters put into exact and clear words the demands that their own soul has heard murmured by its interior Master, and show them how to be faithful to these. The heroism of this asceticism, the spiritual climate into which it introduces them, becomes for them a source of peace and ensures their spiritual balance.[12]

THE NATURE AND PURPOSE OF THE PASSIVE NIGHT OF SENSE

The first chapters of Book One of the *Dark Night* deal with fervent beginners who, because of their love for God, feel that they can reach perfect union with him by their own efforts. To correct this impression, St John devotes seven chapters to the imperfections of beginners. These devastating chapters were not introduced in order to discourage the efforts of beginners, but to clarify the necessity and purpose of the passive night. Thus beginners will be helped "to understand the feebleness of their state and take courage and desire that God place them in this night where the soul is strengthened in virtue and fortified for the inestimable delights of the love of God". It is a merciful intervention of God that puts the soul in this dark night in order to "dry up and purge" all its sensory appetite. "He does not allow it to find sweetness in anything." Instead, he begins to communicate himself through "pure spirit" in contemplation, which St John likens here to the manna in the desert. "This food is the beginning of a contemplation that is dark and dry to the senses." If the soul does not look back but remains without desire for its former sensory satisfactions, it will soon "in that unconcern and idleness delicately experience the interior nourishment".

When souls have practised the virtues for some time and have persevered in prayer, through the sweetness and pleasure they find in these exercises they lose their love for earthly things and gain some degree of strength. They are now able to suffer a light burden of aridity without turning back. Yet their conduct, apparently so perfect, is only a beginning. Even though their pleasure is for spiritual things, it is not far removed from self-love and sense pleasure in other things. God desires to lift them from this lowly manner of loving to one that is more according to the spirit. He will free them from their imperfections and make them capable of a more abundant communion with himself. His method of doing this, however, will not be according to what those fervent beginners were expecting.

Consequently, it is at the time they are going about their spiritual exercises with delight and satisfaction, when in their opinion the sun of divine favor is shining most brightly on them, that God darkens all this light and closes the door and spring of the sweet spiritual water they were tasting as often and as long as they desired. For since they were weak and tender, no door was closed to them, as St John says in the Apocalypse. (Apocalypse 3:8) God now leaves them in such darkness that they do not know which way to turn in their discursive imaginings; they cannot advance a step in meditation, as they used to, now that the interior sensory faculties are engulfed in this night. He leaves them in such dryness that they not only fail to receive satisfaction and pleasure from their spiritual exercises and works, as they formerly did, but also find these exercises distasteful and bitter.[13]

This description of the passive night of sense leaves us in no doubt about its origin. Its cause is the divine action within the soul. Although it is a painful experience, the soul should strive to do its part in purifying itself so as to merit the "divine cure". God will heal it of what through its own efforts it is unable to remedy. No one can be sufficiently disposed for divine union through personal effort alone. God must take over. But the soul must continue in faithfulness and persevering love in spite of the darkness. Obscure purgative contemplation implements the soul's active efforts. It passively causes a deeper denial of self and imparts vigour and warmth of love. It supplants the love of creatures with another and more powerful love. It causes the soul to die to self and to begin "the sweet and delightful love of God".

St John's description is largely psychological. What happens theologically is that God communicates himself to the soul in order to nourish the soul's theological virtues directly himself, supplying them with the sustenance and support they formerly found in the operation of the senses. All our spiritual activity, having God for its object, must be rooted in the theological virtues. Faith is the root of justification. In order to grow and develop, this faith is "lodged in the womb of reason", and operates normally in a human way. Faith develops *humanly* by the exercise of our natural faculties, imagination, memory, and reason, the mutual interchange bringing spiritual satisfaction to the soul. In contemplation God nourishes the theological virtues *divinely*. He frees the interior powers of the soul from dependence on those that are exterior, and submits them to his own direction. In St Teresa's happy phrase, the soul becomes captive, allowing God to imprison it as one who well knows how to be the captive of its lover.

> O Jesus and my Lord. How valuable is Your love to us here. It holds our love so bound that it doesn't allow it the freedom during that time to love anything else but You.[14]

This "ligature" or isolation of the superior part of the soul deprives the senses of the direction they enjoyed from the intellectual faculties. The senses are not yet adapted for this new communication of God and on that account they suffer in the process. But the benefits of a direct self-communication of God outweigh all psychological considerations.

BENEFITS OF THE NIGHT OF SENSE

The passive night of sense is at first a painful experience. St John hastens to dispel the apprehensions of the beginner:

> For it will please and comfort one who treads this path to know that a way seemingly so rough and adverse and contrary to spiritual gratification engenders so many blessings.[15]

All the blessings are summed up in these four: the delight of peace; habitual remembrance of God and solicitude concerning him; cleanness and purity of soul; and the practice of virtue. Considering the many benefits of this night, its trials and aridities are little in comparison.

> Accordingly, a person should not mind if the operation of his faculties are being lost to him; he ought to desire rather that this be done quickly so that he may be no obstacle to the operation of infused contemplation which God is bestowing, that he may receive it with more peaceful plenitude and make room in his spirit for the enkindling and burning of the love

that this dark and secret contemplation bears and communicates to his soul. For contemplation is nothing else than a secret and peaceful and loving inflow of God, which, if not hampered, fires the soul in the spirit of love.[16]

At first, the fire of love is not a very conscious experience but gradually the soul becomes aware of being drawn by love, "fired with love's urgent longings", without knowing how or where this drawing of love originates.

The consequence of love's urgent longings is that the soul "goes out unseen" from the subjection to sense which characterized its meditations. In comparison with infused contemplation, those purely human activities were feeble, limited, and exposed to error. At every step the soul stumbled into innumerable imperfections and much ignorance. Through the aridities of the night the senses become adapted or accommodated to the action of God in the spirit. Peace comes with a new kind of awareness of God's presence in the centre of the soul, and there is an overflow of sweetness to all the faculties. This person is now liberated from sense bondage in prayer and becomes, in St John's language, a "spiritual" person. This is the essential effect of the night of sense. In addition to the essential effect, there are many particular benefits, corresponding roughly to the list of imperfections given in the first seven chapters of the book (I *Dark Night*).

The first and chief benefit that this dry and dark night of contemplation causes is the knowledge of self and of one's own misery. Besides the fact that all the favors God imparts to the soul are ordinarily wrapped in this knowledge, the aridities and voids of the faculties in relation to the abundance previously experienced, and the difficulty encountered in the practice of virtue make the soul recognize its own lowliness and misery, which was not apparent in the time of its prosperity . . .

Now that the soul is clothed in these other garments of labor, dryness, and desolation, and that its former lights have been darkened, it possesses more authentic lights in this most excellent and necessary virtue of self-knowledge. It considers itself to be nothing and finds no satisfaction in self because it is aware that of itself it neither does nor can do anything.

God esteems this lack of self-satisfaction and the dejection a person has about not serving Him more than all former deeds and gratifications, however notable they may have been, since they were the occasion of many imperfections and a great deal of ignorance.[17]

This authentic light on "self" is accompanied by a new awareness of the greatness and transcendence of God. In this twofold light the beginner learns to commune with God "more respectfully and courteously, the way one should always converse with the Most High". The same considerateness also characterizes the soul's attitude to others. Aware of its own wretchedness, it is not even tempted to think it is more advanced than others. Esteem for others increases. Confronted with its own misery, it has no desire to judge others, and will even be willing to be directed and told what to do by anyone at all.

Besides these benefits, innumerable others flow from this dry contemplation. In the midst of these aridities and straits, God frequently communicates to the soul, when it least expects, spiritual sweetness, a very pure love, and a spiritual knowledge which is sometimes most delicate. Each of these communications is more valuable than all the soul previously sought. Yet in the beginning one will not think so because the spiritual inflow is very delicate and the senses do not perceive it.[18]

DURATION OF THE NIGHT OF SENSE

The passive night of sense covers the entire period of transition from meditation to contemplation. The senses remain empty and dry in the passive night because they have no capacity for the purely spiritual gift of contemplation. This incapacity of the senses is the cause of suffering. They continue in this state of dreary distaste until they have been sufficiently purified to partake of the divine gift bestowed upon the spirit. When the work of adaptation is completed the night of sense comes to an end. The soul is now able to "go out" along the road of the spirit, which is that of proficients, "or the way of infused contemplation, in which God Himself pastures and refreshes the soul without any of its own discursive meditation or active help".[19]

How long the soul must remain in the passive night of sense is not possible to say. The trials and temptations are not identical in each case and their length and intensity vary. Much depends upon the greater or lesser amount of imperfection to be purged and the degree of love to which God wills to raise the soul. On these two considerations God humbles the soul with greater or lesser intensity, and for a longer or shorter time.

But those who are very weak He keeps in this night for a long time. Their purgation is less intense and their temptations abated, and He frequently refreshes their senses to keep them from backsliding. They arrive at the purity of perfection late in life. And some of them never reach it entirely, for they are never wholly in the night nor wholly out of it. Although they do not advance, God exercises them for short periods and on certain days in those temptations and aridities to preserve them in humility and self-knowledge; and at other times and seasons He comes to their aid with consolation, lest through loss of courage they return to their search after worldly consolation.[20]

The length of time also varies in the case of those who are afterwards to undergo the more oppressive night of the spirit. For them the night of sense is an integral part of a higher destiny. It is generally a case of burdensome trials and temptations which last a long time "no matter how quickly God leads them".[21]

DARK NIGHTS FOR
ACTIVE CONTEMPLATIVES

It would be easy to gain the impression that when St John writes about the passive nights of sense and spirit he is referring exclusively to the interior life of prayer. His own life however was far from being one of cloistered calm. Many contemplatives for whom prayer and active life are closely linked will know that his understanding of darkness has been of inestimable help to them in interpreting the meaning of pain that has arisen through other events in their lives, but has been no less integral in their journey to God. When St Teresa writes of the trials of the soul she suggests they originate "both within and without", they include scorn and unmerited praise, misunderstanding by those closest to one, rejection by former friends, physical illness.[22] Père Marie-Eugène, a modern Carmelite scholar, wrote that for an active contemplative "it is indeed in the midst of daily life that the battle takes place. Saint John of the Cross owes it to the purity and penetration of his gaze, that he was able to discern the spiritual elements of this drama and abstract them from the rest so as to present them in their essential reality".[23] For such people, "the purification will be made as intense if not more so, because the fire is fed by more personal failures, anxieties about the work of the apostolate, opportunities for humility, hope, and love".[24]

Experience of darkness in life can be transformed into the nights of sense and spirit that bring the soul to God, if it longs for nothing else than to give itself to him, even in the darkness, and so lays the darkness open to the transforming action of his love. Darkness thus transformed will eventually end in the resurrection. St John's own life did not lack opportunities for this kind of transformation.

NOTES

1 I *D.N.*, 7/5, *K.*, p. 311
2 Prologue *D.N.*, *K.*, p. 296
3 Fr Gabriel of St Mary Magdalen OCD, *St John of the Cross*, translated by a Benedictine of Stanbrook, Cork, Mercier Press, 1946, p. 7
4 Hans Urs von Balthasar *The Glory of the Lord*, Volume I, p. 125: *Seeing the Form*, translated by Erasmo Leiva-Merikakis, edited by Joseph Fessio, SJ and John Riches, Edinburgh, T. & T. Clark, 1982
5 Dionysius the Areopagite *The Divine Names* and *Mystical Theology*, translated by C.E. Rolt, London, SPCK, 1940, p. 191–2; (Translation slightly altered)
6 Fr Gabriel of St Mary Magdalen OCD *St John of the Cross*, p. 7
7 Prologue I *D.N.*, *K.*, p. 296
8 Stanza 5, *K.*, p. 296
9 I *D.N.*, Explanation, 1, *K.*, p. 297
10 I. *D.N.*, 8/1, *K.*, p. 311
11 I *D.N.*, 8/2, *K.*, p. 312
12 Père Marie-Eugène OCD *I am a Daughter of the Church: A practical synthesis of Carmelite Spirituality*, translated by Sr M. Verda Clare CSL, Maryland, Christian Classics, 1955, reprinted 1979, p. 126
13 I *D.N.*, 8/3, *K.*, p. 312
14 St Teresa *Life*, 14/2 translated by Kieran Kavanaugh OCD and Otilio Rodriguez OCD, *The Collected Works of St Teresa of Avila*, Washington, D.C., ICS Publications, 1976, vol. I, p. 97
15 I *D.N.*, 11/4, *K.*, p. 320
16 I *D.N.*, 10/6, *K.*, p. 318
17 I *D.N.*, 12/2, *K.*, p. 321
18 I *D.N.*, 13/10, *K.*, p. 326

19   I *D.N.*, 14/1, *K.*, p. 327
20   I *D.N.*, 14/5, *K.*, p. 329
21   I *D.N.*, 14/6, *K.*, p. 329
22   *Mansions* VI, 1
23   Père Marie-Eugène OCD Op. cit., p. 372
24   Ibid., p. 373

13

THE PASSIVE
NIGHT OF SPIRIT

Book II of the *Dark Night* begins by reminding us that if God intends to lead the soul on, he does not place it in the dark night of the spirit immediately after the afflictions and trials of the night of sense. Instead, after having emerged from the state of beginners, the soul usually spends many years exercising itself in the state of proficients.

> In this new state, as one liberated from a cramped prison cell, the soul goes about the things of God with much more freedom and satisfaction of spirit and with more abundant interior delight than it did in the beginning before entering the night of sense. Its imagination and faculties are no longer bound to discursive meditation and spiritual solicitude, as was their custom. The soul readily finds in its spirit, without the work of meditation, a very serene, loving contemplation and spiritual delight.[1]

Nevertheless, even in this happy state, certain needs, aridities, darknesses, and conflicts can be felt occasionally, as omens of the night to come. For the purification of the soul is not yet complete. Former habits of imperfection remain like roots in the spirit that were untouched by the sensory purgation. The sensory purgation was for spiritual integration rather than for immediate union with God. It accommodated the senses to the spirit so that both of them could be purified together and prepared for union.

DARK NIGHT, BOOK II: The Passive Night of the Spirit

The real purgation of the senses begins with the night of the spirit. Both must undergo a complete renewal together, for one part is never cleansed completely without the other. The difference between the two purgations, St John says, is like the difference between pulling up roots and cutting off a branch.

Accordingly, in his account of the night of sense, St John always seemed to be hastening forward to the explanation of the night of the spirit, "for hardly anything has been said of it, in sermons or in writing, and even the experience of it is rare".[2] For the same reason, he abbreviated considerably his treatment of the imperfections of proficients.

> So much could be said about the imperfections of these proficients and of how irremediable they are – since proficients think their blessings are more spiritual than formerly – that I desire to pass over the matter. I only assert, in order to establish the necessity of the spiritual night (the purgation) for anyone who is to advance, that no proficient, however strenuous his efforts, will avoid many of these natural affections and imperfect habits; and these must be purified before he passes on to the divine union.[3]

The night of the spirit completes the story of the soul's journey to perfect union with God.

THE *DARK NIGHT*, BOOK II: SUMMARY

There are twenty-five chapters in this book and, in spite of its title, only three chapters deal with the afflictions of the night. The other chapters describe the benefits of light and love that come to the soul. The commentary is taken up almost entirely with the first two stanzas of the poem. So the book falls naturally into two sections: the soul's renewal in God, and its escape to divine union. In both sections there is a thanksgiving chapter, because of the "sheer grace" of being able to go out in freedom from enemies. The escape is not now from meditation and lowly ways of seeking God, but from all self-seeking that could impede divine union. The section on renewal concentrates on the three faculties of intellect, memory, and will. The reason for this is that, according to St John, union with God is a "union of likeness", that is, a union of the activity of these three faculties with the activity of God. In the high state of perfect union, the soul and God remain as distinct as before, but the soul's knowing and loving become one with the knowing and loving of God. The faculties of the soul, therefore, must be renewed and elevated to the divine level. The experience of this renewal is a painful dark night for the soul. The loving inflow of God purges the soul of its habitual ignorances and imperfections, both spiritual and natural. God does this by means of a dark, obscure contemplation, a mystical theology, a secret wisdom.

> Insofar as infused contemplation is loving wisdom of God, it produces two principal effects in the soul: it prepares the soul for union with God through love by both purging and illumining it. Hence the same loving wisdom that purges and illumines the blessed spirits, purges and illumines the soul here on earth.[4]

St John accordingly subdivided his treatment of renewal into the afflictions of the night and its benefits, the afflictions of purgation and the benefits of illumination.

The second stanza of the poem tells how the escape to divine union took place:

> In darkness, and secure,
> By the secret ladder, disguised
> – Ah, the sheer grace –
> In darkness and concealment,
> My house being now all stilled;

Almost each word in the stanza has a chapter to itself in the commentary (secure, 16; secret, 17; ladder, 18). On the ladder there are ten steps of love (the first five, chapter 19; the second five, chapter 20). The disguise of the soul puts it beyond the reach of Satan (chapter 21). The house of the soul is now at rest because it has discarded all inordinate appetites and desires in preparation for putting on the new bridal veil. Like the bride in the Song of Songs, who found him whom her soul loved, the soul is now safe from the disturbances of Satan and of the senses, and it receives from the divinity itself substantial touches of divine union. "With these touches the soul is purified, quieted, strengthened, and made stable that it may be able to receive permanently this divine union, which is the divine espousal between the soul and the Son of God."[5]

A few characteristics of the night of the spirit are mentioned in a brief commentary on stanza three. And so the book ends.

AFFLICTIONS OF THE NIGHT

Although the loving wisdom of God is divine light it produces not only night and darkness in the soul but also affliction and torment. St John invokes two principles to explain why this happens. The first is taken from Aristotle's *Metaphysics*: the clearer and more obvious divine things are in themselves, the darker and more hidden they are to the soul naturally. "The brighter the light, the more the owl is blinded; and the more one looks at the brilliant sun, the more the sun darkens the faculty of sight, deprives it and overwhelms it in its weakness."[6] The excellence of the divine wisdom exceeds the capacity of the soul which, because of its baseness and imperfection, suffers pain and affliction. The second principle is that two contraries cannot coexist in the same subject. This principle applies only to the extremes which mutually expel each other. Contraries in a modified state can exist together. St John enumerates some of the extremes which make the soul a battlefield. When the extreme of the uncreated perfection of God touches the other extreme of created imperfection, the soul feels that it is being cast away forever from all divine favour.

The soul, because of its impurity, suffers immensely at the time this divine light truly assails it. When this pure light strikes in order to expel all impurity, a person feels so unclean and wretched that it seems God is against him and that he is against God ... Clearly beholding its impurity by means of this pure light, although in darkness, the soul understands distinctly that it is worthy neither of God nor of any creature. And what most grieves it is that it thinks it will never be worthy, and that there are no more blessings for it ... Since this divine contemplation assails him somewhat forcibly in order to subdue and strengthen his soul, he suffers so much in his weakness that he almost dies, particularly at times when the light is more powerful. Both sense and spirit, as though under an immense and dark load, undergo such agony and pain that the soul would consider death a relief ... How amazing and pitiful it is that the soul be so utterly weak and impure that the hand of God, though light and gentle, should feel so heavy and contrary. For the hand of God does not press down or weigh upon the soul, but only touches it; and this mercifully, for God's aim is to grant it favours and not chastise it.[7]

The night of the spirit takes place in the inmost depths of the soul. Since it is produced by divine light, it involves a new level of spiritual awareness on the part of the soul. It does not belong in the realm of the unconscious nor in the subconscious drives of sense appetite. It is genuinely a night of *spirit*. As a conflict of extremes, it is exemplified in a unique way in the agony of Christ in the garden.

> The dark night of the spirit is truly a drama. To get some light on its horror and explain its fruitfulness, one must compare it with the drama of Gethsemane, which it prolongs. Gethsemane was witness to the conflict between the purity of God and the sin of the world, waged in the sacred humanity of Christ who bore that twofold weight. In his humanity he was crushed by it, broken, made into nothingness . . . The night of the spirit is a participation in that suffering and that victory.[8]

St John's comparisons are very striking. They are taken mostly from the psalms, from Job, and the Lamentations of Jeremiah, hints of his own experience surfacing when he describes what the soul "feels" at this time.

> The divine extreme is the purgative contemplation and the human extreme is the soul, the receiver of this contemplation. Since the divine extreme strikes in order to renew the soul and divinize it . . . it so disentangles and dissolves the spiritual substance – absorbing it in profound darkness – that the soul at the sight of its miseries feels that it is melting away and being undone by a cruel spiritual death . . . It is fitting that the soul be in this sepulchre of dark death in order that it attain the spiritual resurrection for which it hopes.[9]

Contemplation is sometimes compared to fire, the biblical image for inward cleansing as distinct from the outward washing of water. Just as fire consumes the rust of metal, contemplation annihilates and consumes all the imperfect habits the soul had contracted throughout its life. Since these imperfections are deeply rooted in the substance of the soul, their cleansing is an oppressive experience in the inward depths of the spirit.

But what the sorrowing soul feels most is the conviction that God has rejected it, and with an abhorrence of it cast it into darkness. The thought that God has abandoned it is a piteous and heavy affliction for the soul ... When this purgative contemplation oppresses a man, he feels very vividly indeed the shadow of death, the sighs of death, and the sorrows of hell, all of which reflect the feeling of God's absence, of being chastised and rejected by Him, and of being unworthy of Him, as well as the object of His anger. The soul experiences all this and even more, for now it seems that this affliction will last forever.[10]

Perhaps St John's personal experience is reflected in his plea that one ought to have deep compassion for the soul God places in this night. The soul is fortunate because of the sublime work God is accomplishing in it. "Nevertheless the soul is deserving of great pity because of the immense tribulation it suffers and its extreme uncertainty about a remedy." No doctrine or spiritual direction can be a support or consolation to it at this time.

Instead of consolation he experiences greater sorrow thinking that the director's doctrine is no remedy for his evil. Indeed, it is not a remedy, for until the Lord finishes purging him in the way He desires, no remedy is a help to him in his sorrow. His helplessness is even greater because of the little he can do in this situation. He resembles one who is imprisoned in a dark dungeon, bound hands and feet, and able neither to move, nor see, nor feel any favor from heaven or earth. He remains in this condition until his spirit is humbled, softened, and purified, until it becomes so delicate, simple, and refined that it can be one with the Spirit of God, according to the degree of union of love that God, in His mercy, desires to grant. In conformity with this degree, the purgation is of greater or lesser force and endures for a longer or shorter time.[11]

RENEWAL OF THE SOUL IN GOD

A final comparison used by St John sums up his teaching: purgative contemplation has the same effect on the soul as fire on a log of wood. The soul is prepared for union with God just as wood, on an older understanding, is prepared for transformation into fire. Fire first expels the moisture, then makes the wood black and ugly and causes it to give out smoke. The fire cleanses the wood of these ugly, dark qualities and transforms it into itself, making it as beautiful as itself. It now possesses the properties and performs the action of fire. So, St John says, should we philosophize about the divine, loving fire of contemplation. "With this example in mind . . . it will be a good thing to leave these sad experiences and begin now to discuss the fruit of the soul's tears."[12]

In the night of spirit, the fire of love penetrates the soul's depths. Unlike love's urgent longings of the senses, the effect here is a profound interior cleansing and renewal, as different from the night of sense as is the soul from the body.

For this enkindling of love occurs in the spirit and through it the soul in the midst of these dark conflicts feels vividly and keenly that it is being wounded by a strong divine love, and it has a certain feeling and foretaste of God. Yet it understands nothing in particular, for as we said the intellect is in darkness. The spirit herein experiences an impassioned and intense love, because this spiritual inflaming engenders the passion of love. Since this love is infused, it is more passive than active and thus generates in the soul a strong passion of love. This love is now beginning to possess something of union with God and thereby shares to a certain extent in its properties. These properties are actions of God more than of the soul and they reside in it passively, although the soul does give its consent.[13]

The consequence of this passion of love is similar to what happens in any human "passion". It drains out on its own behalf all the energies and strength of the other faculties and powers. When a person is the victim of an evil "passion", then reputation, property, friends, and physical well-being are all sacrificed on the altar of this one craving. Similarly, when the soul is "wounded" and impassioned with divine love, all its strength and appetites are recollected in this burning of love.

One might, then, in a certain way ponder how remarkable and how strong this enkindling of love in the spirit can be. God gathers together all the strength, faculties, and appetites of the soul, spiritual and sensory alike, that the energy and power of this whole harmonious composite may be employed in this love. The soul consequently arrives at the true fulfilment of the first commandment which, neither disdaining anything human nor excluding it from this love, states: "*You shall love your God with your whole heart and with your whole mind and with your whole soul and with all your strength.*" (Deuteronomy 6: 5)[14]

Love has this characteristic: everything seems possible to it. It believes everyone is occupied as it is itself, and it does not believe that anyone could be employed in any other way or seek anyone other than God whom it seeks and loves. It believes there is nothing else to desire. The soul, wounded with love, goes out "anxiously and forcibly" in search of its God. When the soul was in its purgative darkness, it could see only its own misery and unworthiness. How does it now have this new energy and daring to go out towards union with God? The first reason is that even though this purifying night darkens the spirit, it does so only to impart light concerning all things. It humbles only to exalt. It deprives the soul of all possessions only that it "may reach out *divinely* to the enjoyment of all earthly and heavenly things, with a general spirit of freedom in them all".[15] The second reason for the soul's daring is the nature of love itself which always seeks union. The soul's longing to be "united, joined, equalled, and assimilated to the loved object" imparts strength and daring beyond the soul's natural capacity. It was the function of the night of the spirit to divinize the faculties of the soul, and so equip them for the exalted state of union. The soul calls it a "sheer grace" because a work of renovation has been wrought in it which, like resurrection from death, could be brought about only by God.

> This renovation is: an illumination of the human intellect with supernatural light so that it becomes divine, united with the divine; an informing of the will with love of God so that it is no longer less than divine and loves in no other way than divinely, united and made one with the divine will and love; and also a divine conversion and change of the memory, the affections, and the appetites according to God. And thus this soul will be a soul of heaven, heavenly and more divine than human.[16]

THE ESCAPE

If the angels rejoice over a sinner who repents, the same must be true of a soul that reaches divine union. Seen in the divine light the adventure is an exciting escape-story. Some of the excitement comes through in St John's account of it. He seems to take delight in proving that the happy outcome of union is the direct result of the dark night, even though the actual experience of the night creates a contrary impression.

> . . . we should not think a person runs a more serious risk of being lost because of the torments of anguish, the doubts, the fears, and the horrors of this night and darkness, for rather a man is saved in the darkness of this night. In this night the soul

subtly escapes from its enemies, who are always opposed to its departure.[17]

Unlike the angels whose decisions remain unchanged forever, the human soul has a certain mobility through its passions and appetites. By these it may fail through excess or defect; it may change or go astray. It can become its own enemy through its appetites. Once all these movements of appetite are impeded, the soul is obviously freed from error in them, and liberated from self and from its other enemies, the world and the devil.[18] In the dark night the soul is secure from vainglory, from pride and presumption, and from many other evils. It is a singular grace when the appetites are frustrated, the inclinations constrained and dry, and the faculties incapacitated for any interior activity. For then God is transforming the merely human activity into something much more elevated. For St John of the Cross, the mystery of God is unknown territory. To reach it the soul cannot be guided by its own knowledge, but must walk in darkness by new and unfamiliar paths. The experience may be that of getting lost. "Indeed, it is getting lost to what it knew and tasted, and going by a way in which it neither tastes nor knows."[19] Yet because of the divine intervention, the soul was never as secure,

> With no other light or guide
> Than the one that burned in my heart.

THE SECRET LADDER

St John's description of the "secrecy" of dark contemplation represents one of his clearest insights into the nature of mystical theology. He gives a number of reasons why it is called "secret". The experience itself is ineffable, the path to it unknowable. Divine things are not known as they are in themselves while they are being sought, but only when they are already found. One advances towards them by not knowing rather than by knowing. In addition, mystical wisdom is "secret" because it has the characteristic of hiding the soul within itself.

> Besides its usual effect, this mystical wisdom will occasionally so engulf a person in its secret abyss that he will have the keen awareness of being brought into a place far removed from every creature. He will accordingly feel that he has been led into a remarkably deep and vast wilderness, unattainable by any human creature, into an immense, unbounded desert, the more delightful, savorous, and loving, the deeper, vaster, and more solitary it is.[20]

This secret wisdom is called a ladder, for by a secret contemplation the soul ascends in order "to plunder, know, and possess the goods and treasures of heaven". A ladder is used for ascent and descent. Secret contemplation exalts the soul in God and humbles it within itself, for there are many ups and downs in the spiritual journey. Yet the ladder of contemplation reaches up even to God himself. "For He is at the end of the ladder and it is in Him that the ladder rests."[21]

The chief reason for calling contemplation a ladder is that it is a science of love, "an infused, loving knowledge, that both illumines and enamours the soul, elevating it step by step unto God, its Creator". The steps of love here are not a list of the degrees of charity, but a description of the more elevated regions which the soul climbs in order to embrace God. There is the sickness of love, the search for God in all things, the many great works done for love of him. The soul thinks these works are very few, like Jacob's seven years' toil, which seemed little to him because of the greatness of his love. A delight in suffering for the Beloved is rewarded by a God-given daring which the soul needs in order to move forward to divine union. "The soul is ever believing that it is finding its Beloved; and when it sees its desire frustrated, which is at almost every step, it faints in its long-ing."[22] The eighth step of love impels the soul to lay hold of the Beloved without letting him go. The ninth step is that of the perfect soul, burning gently with love under the influence of the Holy Spirit. "We cannot speak of the goods and riches of God a man enjoys on this step, because even if we were to write many books about them, the greater part would remain unsaid."[23] After reaching the ninth step in this life, the soul departs from the body. The tenth and last step of the ladder assimilates the soul to God completely because of the clear beatific vision which a person possesses as soon as he or she reaches it. On this last step of clear vision at the top of the ladder where God rests, nothing is any longer hidden from the soul.

NOTES

1   II *D.N.*, 1/1, *K.*, p. 329–30
2   I *D.N.*, 8/2, *K.*, p. 312
3   II *D.N.*, 2/4, *K.*, p. 332
4   II *D.N.*, 5/1, *K.*, p. 335
5   II *D.N.*, 24/3, *K.*, p. 387
6   II *D.N.*, 5/3, *K.*, p. 335
7   II *D.N.*, 5/5, 6, 7, *K.*, p. 336–7
8   Père Marie-Eugène OCD *I am a Daughter of the Church: A practical synthesis of Carmelite spirituality*, translated by Sr M. Verda Clare, CSL Maryland, Christian Classics, 1955, reprinted 1979, p. 126–7
9   II *D.N.*, 6/1, *K.*, p. 337
10   II *D.N.*, 6/3, *K.*, p. 338
11   II *D.N.*, 7/3, *K.*, p. 341–2
12   II *D.N.*, 10/10, *K.*, p. 352
13   II *D.N.*, 11/1, 2, *K.*, p. 352–3
14   II *D.N.*, 11/4, *K.*, p. 353
15   II *D.N.*, 9/1, *K.*, p. 346
16   II *D.N.*, 13/11, *K.*, p. 361

17 II *D.N.*, 15/1, *K.*, p. 363
18 II *D.N.*, 16/2, *K.*, p. 363
19 II *D.N.*, 16/8, *K.*, p. 365
20 II *D.N.*, 17/6, *K.*, p. 370
21 II *D.N.*, 18/4, *K.*, p. 372
22 II *D.N.*, 19/5, *K.*, p. 375
23 II *D.N.*, 20/4, *K.*, p. 377

14

THE SPIRITUAL
CANTICLE

The *Spiritual Canticle* is regarded by many as the greatest of St John of the Cross's writings. It opens for us the journey of love just as the *Ascent-Night* opens the journey of faith. The poem was conceived and most of its stanzas were written while John was in the Toledo prison, without books or much light for reading. Its similarity to the Song of Solomon reveals how St John's memory was furnished. He may even have known the Song by heart, for it was his favourite piece of Scripture. His recollection of it came readily to mind when he was trying to express the exchange of love between Christ and himself. The biblical imagery was an apt vehicle for his purpose. St John was now a fully integrated person, and his poetic creativity would be perfected by his mystical endowment. In fact, St John became more than anything else the poet of divine love, and incidentally, "the loftiest poet of Spain". However, it was not the poetic dimension of the Song of Solomon that captured St John's attention, but the fact that it was

the poetry *par excellence* of the love of Christ and ourselves, a poetry that is bold enough to put into words the things we experience but scarcely dare to name: our longing for Christ and his longing for us, our terror when we call and do not find him, and the profound tranquillity of the union into which he invites us.[1]

THE TRADITION OF BRIDAL MYSTICISM

At the time of St John of the Cross, tradition had accepted the Song of Solomon as the inspired expression of bridal mysticism. Many early commentators, including Origen, favoured this interpretation. St Jerome, an admirer of Origen's commentaries, said that Origen, who surpassed all men in his other writings, surpassed himself in the Song of Songs.[2] One is tempted to give a similar verdict on St John of the Cross's *Spiritual Canticle*. It certainly sustains a very exalted level of religious writing, and as we turn over its pages we know that we have entered the holy of holies.[3] We are not surprised to hear that St John wrote some at least of the commentary on the *Spiritual Canticle* on his knees.

Origen's interpretation of the Song sees in Solomon the figure of Christ, either the Church or the loving soul being the bride. "This allegory strongly influenced all later exegesis in the West and survived in the mysticism of the middle ages."[4] St John of the Cross follows the allegorical interpretation of Origen, but applies his *Canticle* almost exclusively to Christ and the individual loving soul, taking for granted that the individual is not isolated but a member of the Church. An extremist of the Antioch school, founded in opposition to the allegorical method of Origen, held that the Song was in fact "an epithalamium composed by Solomon to celebrate his marriage with the Egyptian princess".[5] This literal interpretation finds some favour with modern exegetes, but it does not exclude the application of the Song to Christ and the loving soul. The union of marriage was adopted in the Old Testament as the nearest appropriate image of God's love for his people. The theme first appeared in Hosea, and was later resumed in Isaiah, Jeremiah and Ezechiel.[6] The gospels describe the messianic days as a wedding feast, and St Paul speaks of Christ as the Bridegroom with the Church as the pure bride married to her one husband. The Apocalypse celebrates the wedding feast of the Lamb at the final consummation of all things.

The union of the soul with Christ in contemplation was not commonly spoken of as "marriage" until the time of St Bernard. His commentaries on the Song of Songs gave impetus to all the subsequent development of bridal mysticism.

> I cannot contain myself for joy that the Divine Majesty disdains not to stoop to a familiar and sweet companionship with our lowliness, nor the supernal Godhead to enter into a marriage with a soul still in exile, and despises not to show it the affection of a bridegroom possessed of a most ardent love.[7]

Frequent reference to Christ and the individual soul may create the impression of spiritual selfishness, we are so accustomed nowadays to the community dimension. This would be to miss the whole wavelength of the mystics. For the precise purpose of the obscure night of contemplation is to liberate the soul from selfishness, spiritual or otherwise. When it thus enters into communion with God, it is in communion also with all creation. The ascent to God requires departure from self, and it is only the gift of contemplation that enables a person to achieve it. "By means of this mystical theology and secret love, the soul departs from itself and all things and ascends to God."[8] From this eminence the soul enjoys an expansive world-view, embracing the whole community of people upon earth, with a foretaste of the community of the blessed.

> The love of the Bridegroom, far from enclosing one in an intimacy that shuts out the rest of the world, is always opened in the Song, as in the entire mystical tradition, to the entire universe. The closest union with the Bridegroom has this consequence: it always puts one in communion with the world and with all mankind . . . Though nothing is more personal,

160

more intimate than the Song, nothing is either more universal and more cosmic.[9]

In the end it is an ever more real and widespread spiritual society that must be rediscovered in the deepest, most abandoned interior silence.[10]

THE SOUL GOES OUT IN SEARCH OF THE BELOVED

Before beginning his commentary, St John describes the stanzas of the *Spiritual Canticle* as "love songs between the bride and Christ, the Bridegroom". They were the spontaneous expression of St John's own love for Christ, "obviously composed with a certain burning love of God".[11] Poetry was more appropriate for the celebration of his love than the calculated restrictions of prose. Therefore, in the prose commentary, St John does not confine the reader to a precise, limited understanding of the stanzas, but rather suggests a meaning in order to share with us his own experience of divine love.

It would be foolish to think that expressions of love arising from mystical understanding, like these stanzas, are fully explainable ... For mystical wisdom, which comes through love and is the subject of these stanzas, need not be understood distinctly in order to cause love and affection in the soul, for it is given according to the mode of faith, through which we love God without understanding Him.[12]

This means that the *Spiritual Canticle*, with its commentary, is an open book for all, each one deriving profit from it "according to the mode and capacity of his spirit".[13]

The subject of the stanzas is mystical wisdom. But the

commentary includes some lengthy explanations concerning prayer and its effects, since these are referred to in the poem. The commentary was addressed to Mother Ann of Jesus, prioress of the Carmelite nuns in Granada, who had been led "beyond the state of beginners into the depths of His divine love".[14] She would therefore appreciate some scholastic theology in the commentary, for the truths understood by the theologians are events in the life-experience of the mystics. What is proclaimed publicly in the Creed may become "secret wisdom" in the heart of the believer. These events of mystical wisdom are so wonderful that St John often appeals to sacred Scripture to make them credible.

A frequent cause of wonder in the mystical life is the way the Bridegroom suddenly "shows and then hides Himself", like the stag on a distant hill. This was the experience of the bride at the beginning of St John's *Canticle*: "You fled like the stag / After wounding me." It is well to note that the wound of love is not the bride's alone. "Beholding that the bride is wounded with love for Him, He also, because of her moan, is wounded with love for her. Among lovers, the wound of one is a wound for both."[15] But the stag that suddenly appears "on the hill" just as suddenly vanishes. Thus the drama of the *Canticle* begins. The bride, wounded with love, goes out in search of the Beloved calling after him, but he has gone.

St John does not tell us how this wounding of the soul took place. He merely gives us the headings of certain meditations which served as a preparation for it. This long list of considerations gathers momentum as the point of decision approaches.

Renouncing all things, leaving aside all business, and not delaying a day or an hour, with desires and sighs pouring from her heart, wounded now with love for God, she begins to call her Beloved and say: "Where have you hidden, / Beloved, and left me moaning? . . . I went out calling You, and You were gone."

Thus the stage is set for the journey of love.

The terminus of the journey is the spiritual marriage, the ultimate state of perfection. But even in the first stanzas the longing of the soul is so intense that only the union of the next life can satisfy it. "In this first stanza the soul, enamoured of the Word, her Bridegroom, the Son of God, longs for union with Him through clear and essential vision."[16] The reason the soul has this intense longing is that, even at this early stage, "she has departed from all creatures and from herself", and yet must suffer her Beloved's absence. St John distinguishes two ways of "going out" after God. One consists of a departure from all things created, since they have lost their attractiveness for the soul; the other is a forgetfulness of self because of the love of God. The wound of love causes the soul to "go out" in these two ways.

> When the love of God really touches the soul, as we are saying, it so raises her up that it not only impels her to go out from self in this forgetfulness, but even draws her away from her natural supports, manners, and inclinations, thus inducing her to call after God.[17]

Even though there is a certain continuity between the *Ascent-Night* and the *Spiritual Canticle*, yet when we open the *Canticle* we feel that we have entered a new world. The bride "is longing for union with the divinity of the Word, her Bridegroom".[18] Bemoaning his absence, she has "gone out" in search of him. To say that the *Ascent-Night* represents the journey of faith and the *Canticle* the journey of love is merely a matter of emphasis, for faith and love are together all the way to union with

God. St John compares faith to the feet; love is the guide.[19] The exciting feature of the *Canticle*, as distinct from the *Ascent-Night*, is that we are now on the way to a discovery of the content of faith. Love reveals the secrets of the heart.

> In dealing with these mysteries and secrets of faith, the soul will merit through love the discovery of the content of faith, that is, the Bridegroom whom she desires to possess in this life through the special grace of divine union with God, as we said, and in the next through the essential glory.[20]

The distinguishing feature of the *Canticle* is God's new mystical presence to the soul, by which he begins to reveal himself. The bride who has "gone out" in search of the Beloved will find him. St Thomas teaches that

> God is in all things by His power, inasmuch as all things are subject to His power; He is by His presence in all things as all things are bare and open to His eyes; He is in all things by His essence, inasmuch as He is present to all as the cause of their being.[21]

These three ways together are the common mode of divine presence, which St Thomas distinguishes from the special mode, by which God is said "to be present more familiarly in some by grace". St John of the Cross follows this teaching when he says that God is present by essence and by grace, but he adds a third mode, "His presence by spiritual affection, for God usually grants (manifests) His spiritual presence to devout souls in many ways, by which He refreshes, delights, and gladdens them".[22] By this presence we might say that the mystical life proper has begun and the soul is feeling its way from grace to glory. "As He gives the soul natural being through His essential presence, and perfects her through His presence by grace, she begs Him to glorify her also with His manifest glory."[23]

The special mode of divine presence which characterizes the *Canticle* also reveals God's absence, and thus introduces the painful and loving search. St John carries the drama forward by telling the bride where her Beloved may be found.

> The Word, the Son of God, together with the Father and the Holy Ghost, is hidden by His essence and His presence in the innermost being of the soul . . . and there the good contemplative must seek Him with love . . . Oh then, soul, most beautiful among all the creatures, so anxious to know the dwelling place of your Beloved that you may go in quest of Him and be united with Him, now we are telling you that you yourself are His dwelling and His secret chamber and hiding place.[24]

The dialogue of St John and the soul is here skilfully arranged so that the Saint's favourite doctrine of interior recollection can be emphasized. For the soul naturally asks the question, "Since He whom my soul loves is within me, why don't I find Him or experience Him?" St John's reply is the key to many questions that might be asked about the *Canticle*, and it states the obvious ascetical principle of the search for a hidden God.

> Anyone who is to find a hidden treasure must enter the hiding place secretly, and once he has discovered it, he will also be hidden just as the treasure is hidden. Since, then, your beloved Bridegroom is the treasure hidden in a field . . . and that field is your soul, in order to find Him you should forget all your possessions and all creatures and hide in the interior, secret chamber of your spirit . . . Remaining hidden with Him, you will experience Him in hiding, and love and enjoy Him in hiding, and you will delight with Him in hiding, that is, in a way transcending all language and feeling.[25]

IN SOLITUDE FOR HER BELOVED'S SAKE

Solitude and recollection are often mentioned in St John's writings as basic requirements for advancing in the spiritual life. The dark night of obscure contemplation, "the mystical theology which theologians call secret wisdom", hides the soul in its interior recollection. It is called "secret" because it is indescribable, and also "because it has the characteristic of hiding the soul within itself. Besides its usual effect, this mystical wisdom will occasionally so engulf a person in its secret abyss that he will have a keen awareness of being brought into a place far removed from every creature".[26] This mystical grace of solitude may be prepared for by the soul's own efforts, or by providential circumstances like illness, bereavement, or misunderstandings and estrangement of friends. It can also be hindered. In a section of the *Living Flame*, called St John's "mystical summa",[27] it is shown how the devil can easily draw the soul out of its recollection by keeping a number of "good things" in fashion on the religious market. He intrudes on the soul's withdrawal

> with some clouds of knowledge and sensible satisfaction. This knowledge and the satisfaction he gives is sometimes good, so that he may feed the soul more and make it turn to this good knowledge and satisfaction, embrace it and journey to God leaning upon it ... Since in that solitude and quiet of the faculties, the soul was doing nothing, it seems that this way is better because it is now doing something ... He makes the soul lose abundant riches by alluring it with a little bait – as one would allure a fish – out of the simple waters of the spirit.[28]

The presence of God characteristic of the *Canticle* presupposes solitude. Only when the soul hides itself in its interior recollection is it open for the affective or spiritual presence of

God as manifestation. St John is not here framing an argument for an ascetical practice, but simply stating the fact that this is the way love acts, since "love is a union between two alone".[29] Solitude was the means used by the soul to find and rejoice in her Beloved alone. The Bridegroom therefore

> bears a great love for the solitude of the soul; but He is wounded much more by her love, since being wounded with love for Him, she desired to live alone in respect to all things. And He does not wish to leave her alone, but wounded by the solitude she embraces for His sake, and observing that she is dissatisfied with any other thing, He alone guides her, drawing her to and absorbing her in Himself. Had He not found her in spiritual solitude, He would not have wrought this in her.[30]

Spiritual solitude and the "spiritual presence" of God are correlatives. Just as spiritual solitude is a foretaste or rehearsal for the final withdrawal from all things at death, so the "spiritual presence" of God is a foretaste of the full vision of God in heaven. This occurs in the third part of the night, referred to by St John in the early pages of the *Ascent*. Whereas faith is a dark night like midnight, "the third part, representing God, is like the very early dawn just before the break of day".[31] This may show, incidentally, that when St John began the *Ascent* he had already conceived his four major works as one systematic whole. The "spiritual presence" of the *Canticle* takes the soul to the threshold of eternity.

> This presence is so sublime that the soul feels an immense hidden being is there from which God communicates to her some semi-clear glimpses of His divine beauty. And these bear such an effect on the soul that she ardently longs and faints with desire for what she feels hidden there in that

presence . . . the soul faints with longing to be ungulfed in that supreme good.[32]

The suffering and pain from this keen perception of God can be very intense, especially in those who are near perfection, so intense "that if God did not provide, they would die . . . For an immense good is shown them, as through the fissure of a rock, but not granted them. Thus their pain and torment is unspeakable".[33] Unlike the sufferings of the dark night, the pain here is not the result of a conflict between the imperfect condition of the soul and the excellence of God. It is caused by the special grace of being drawn towards and at the same time being hindered from an infinite good. The nearer the soul comes to God the greater is her experience of his absence. This void is like a spiritual fire "which dries up and purges her, so that thus purified she may be united with Him".[34]

This is more than the restlessness of love. The soul now lives more in the next life than in this, and has little esteem for this temporal life. "He who is in love is said to have his heart stolen or seized by the object of his love."[35] The soul cannot now direct its love towards any other object, nor find satisfaction in anything but God. Until it gains possession of him, the soul is like an empty vessel waiting to be filled, or like a hungry man craving for food. In everything he sees and hears he has only one desire.[36]

But God, the loving Bridegroom of souls, cannot watch this soul suffering very long alone, especially since these sufferings are the outcome of love for him.[37]

SPIRITUAL BETROTHAL

St John describes spiritual betrothal at its maximum. Not all souls are equally privileged. To some God gives more, to some less; to some in one way, to some in another. The prominent elements in this betrothal are the height of contemplation and the flight of the soul in rapture.

> God is in sight on the hill ... For contemplation is a high place where God in this life begins to communicate and show Himself to the soul, but not completely. However sublime may be the knowledge God gives the soul in this life, it is but a glimpse of Him from a great distance.[38]

Yet this knowledge has such a profound effect on the bride-soul that while she still dwells in the body she lives with "the driving force of a fathomless desire for union with God".[39]

The intense longings of the soul are the preparation for God's gracious manifestation of himself. He now communicates some rays of light from himself "with such strong love and glory" that her bodily condition is not able to support it. "The Beloved revealed to her some rays of His grandeur and divinity. He communicated these so sublimely and forcibly that He carried her out of herself in rapture and ecstasy."[40] Her spirit is elevated to commune with the divine Spirit, and so "the soul must in some fashion abandon the body". The divine communication is so abundant that a person receives it almost at the cost of life. Body and soul both suffer when the spirit takes flight in this special form of supernatural recollection.

The cause of rapture in the state of spiritual espousal is that the soul is raised to a level of knowledge and love of God beyond the reach of the senses. The bride-soul had been longing and yearning for the "divine eyes", but when they looked upon her, it was more than she could endure. St John represents her as saying, "Withdraw them Beloved ... for they cause me to take flight and go out of myself to supreme contemplation, which is beyond what the sensory part can endure".[41] In these visits, God manifests such wonderful truths about himself that the soul longs for death in order to be united to the grandeur and beauty revealed to her. It is an imperfection to desire death, and if the soul could enjoy God without dying she would not want death. But the attractive power of what she beholds sets up a corresponding intense desire to attain it.

> The soul does nothing outstanding by wanting to die at the sight of the beauty of God in order to enjoy Him forever. Were she to have but a foreglimpse of the height and beauty of God, she would not only desire death in order to see Him now forever, as she here desires, but she would very gladly undergo a thousand singularly bitter deaths to see Him only for a moment; and having seen Him, she would ask to suffer just as many more that she might see Him for another moment.[42]

God does not fulfil the soul's desire for death. Instead, he heals the bodily weakness that cannot take his abundant spiritual communications without ecstasy. He conforms the senses to the level of the spirit, bringing tranquillity and peace. In addition, he makes the soul beautiful by participation in his own beauty, adorns her with gifts and virtues, and clothes her with the grandeur and majesty of God himself, as one dressed for betrothal. Under the divine rays, the soul sees not only something of the beauty of God, but also her own supernatural endowment of graces, which are the jewels and adornment for the betrothal. Moreover, the Holy Spirit touches these perfections of the soul in such a way that "they of themselves afford the soul a wonderful fragrance".[43] The dialogue of love now changes its character. There is no more talk of painful longings, but of communion and exchange of sweet and peaceful love.

Having been thus duly prepared, the bride is introduced to the state of spiritual marriage.

SPIRITUAL MARRIAGE

St John opens his account of the spiritual marriage on a note of unclouded joy. God's desire to free the soul is now fulfilled. He rejoices and makes the saints and the angels rejoice with him. "He calls the soul His crown, His bride, and the joy of His heart, and He takes her now in His arms and goes forth with her as the bridegroom from his bridal chamber."[44] The nuptial symbolism helps St John to bring out some of the excellences of this state. Marriage means mutual surrender of persons, delight in each other's company, common possessions, sharing of secrets, equality of love, unity of decision. In the spiritual marriage of the soul and God, all these elements feature in an extraordinary degree. In very exalted language, St John describes what this state of perfect union means and the amazing intimacy of friendship that takes place between the Almighty and his creature.

> It is a total transformation in the Beloved in which each surrenders the entire possession of self to the other with a certain consummation of the union of love. The soul thereby becomes divine, becomes God through participation, insofar as is possible in this life. And thus I think that this state never occurs without the soul's being confirmed in grace, for the faith of both is confirmed when God's faith in the soul is here confirmed. It is accordingly the highest state attainable in this life.[45]

St John of the Cross is not the only mystical writer to associate total transformation of the soul with the state of perfect union. Our Lord once said to St Catherine of Siena, "If anyone should ask me who this soul is, I would reply, She is another myself become so by union of love".[46]

In this soul, then, the covenant between God and the human

race has reached perfection. The marriage prophesies of Hosea, Jeremiah, and Isaiah, already fulfilled in Christ, are extended to another individual. In the language of Blessed Elizabeth of the Trinity, there is now another humanity in which Christ can renew all his mysteries. This can take place because the faith of both is confirmed. "Neither fails the other in anything."[47] God has absolute trust in the soul, and the soul's whole trust is in God. Under this aspect, the spiritual marriage is more like golden jubilee than wedding day. All the doubts and anxieties of love have vanished. This is the final and perfect state. The bride has left behind "everything temporal and natural and all spiritual affections, modes, and manners, and has set aside and forgotten all temptations, disturbances, pains, solicitude, and cares, and is transformed in this high embrace".[48]

Doubts and anxieties have vanished because perfect love does not keep anything hidden from the beloved.

> In this high state of spiritual marriage the Bridegroom reveals His wonderful secrets to the soul, as to His faithful consort, with remarkable ease and frequency. He communicates to her, mainly, sweet mysteries of His Incarnation and of the ways of the Redemption of mankind, which is one of the loftiest of His works, and thus more delightful to the soul.[49]

The great secret of God, hidden from all ages, and revealed in Christ, is now experienced by this privileged soul, causing the greatest love. By this love God makes the soul equal to himself.

> For the property of love is to make the lover equal to the object loved. Since the soul in this state possesses perfect love, she is called the bride of the Son of God, which signifies equality with Him. In this equality of friendship the possessions of both are held in common ... and He is surrendered to all her desires.[50]

When a soul is perfect in love, all her senses, affections, desires, appetites, and other energies are transformed. The soul no longer reaps any disordered self-satisfaction from their activity. The soul "does not rejoice except in God, nor hope in anything other than God; she fears only God and has no sorrow unless in relation to Him."[51] Everything leads the soul to love, and her one pleasure in all things is the delight of loving God. Though the equality of friendship between the soul and God is not as perfect as it will be in the next life, the soul even while on earth is raised to a divine level of loving. Just as God is all love, so also

> this soul that is now perfect is all love, if one may express it so, and all her actions love; she employs all her faculties and possessions in loving, giving up everything, like the wise merchant (Matthew 13: 44), for the treasure of love she has found hidden in God.[52]

Not only is the soul all loving, she is also lovely and attractive in the eyes of God, since he has "arrayed her in His grace and clothed her in His beauty".[53] Oblivious of her former ugliness and the inferiority of her nature, God "loves her ineffably . . . And as He continues to honour and exalt her, He becomes continually more captivated by and enamoured of her".[54] The spiritual marriage and transformation of the soul abide as a permanent state, though not always in act. Yet the resultant activity of love and its varied expressions are very frequent. "The endearing expressions of love which frequently pass between the two are indescribable. She praises and thanks Him, and He extols, praises and thanks her. There are many other expressions of gratitude and praise they repeat to each other."[55]

Since love naturally expresses itself in song, St John represents the Bridegroom as telling in song about the soul's purity in this state and her riches and reward for preparing herself to come to him. He also tells of her good fortune in having found her Bridegroom in this union, and of the fulfilment of her desires and of the delight and refreshment she possesses in him.[56] The bride feels that this voice of her Bridegroom speaking within her is the end of all evil and the beginning of all good.

> Renewing and refreshing the substance of the soul with the sweetness and mellowness of His voice, He calls her as He would call one now disposed to make the journey to eternal life. She too sings a new and jubilant song together with God, Who moves her to do this. He gives His voice to her, that so united with Him she may give it to Him. Such is the song of the soul in the transformation that is hers in this life, the delight of which is beyond all exaggeration. Yet since this song is not as perfect as the new song of the glorious life, the soul in this bliss becomes mindful of the new song of glory, hearing faintly in the song of this life, the excellence of the possession of glory, which is incomparably more precious.[57]

THE BEAUTY OF GOD

The *Spiritual Canticle* might have come to an end with stanza thirty-five (stanza 34 of first redaction). But another five stanzas were added almost by accident, to crown what had already been written. The story is told that when St John of the Cross was confessor to the Carmelite nuns of Beas, he asked Francesca de la Madre de Dios, "In what does prayer consist?" She replied, "In looking at the beauty of God and rejoicing that he has it". Her answer must have corresponded to a special grace the Saint himself had received, for "he began to speak in a wonderful way about uncreated beauty, which was then his favourite subject for days on end, terminating in the composition of the last five verses of his *Spiritual Canticle* begun in the Toledo prison."[58]

In these last five stanzas, the earthly bride longs for the marriage of the beatific state, when the veil of her enlightened faith will give way under the light of glory to the contemplation of God's beauty. Beauty is the final resting place and fulfilment of the mind, and contemplation by its very nature and essence is related to beauty.[59] The journey of faith and the journey of love now become one in St John's contemplation of the beauty of God. More than in the other stanzas, his language here flows from abundant mystical understanding (Prologue 1). Even in the commentary, his words of "explanation" read like an ecstatic utterance:

> I shall see You in Your beauty, and You shall see me in Your beauty, and I shall see myself in You in Your Beauty, and You will see Yourself in me in Your beauty; that I may resemble You in Your beauty, and You resemble me in Your beauty, and my beauty be Your beauty and Your beauty be my beauty; wherefore I shall be You in Your beauty, and You will be me in Your beauty, because Your very beauty will be my beauty; and therefore we shall behold each other in Your beauty.[60]

Beauty adds something to truth and goodness. It is the splendour of their harmony, causing admiration and delight in the whole person. Clarity and due proportion are its foundations. God is said to be beautiful, as being the cause of the harmony and clarity of the universe.[61] Supreme Beauty is the cause of all the beauty of the created world. The transformed soul that has now reached the final revelation of the content of its faith beholds

> the grace, wisdom and beauty which every earthly and heavenly creature not only has from God but also manifests in its wise, well-ordered, gracious and harmonious relationship to other creatures ... The knowledge of this harmony fascinates and delights the soul.[62]

With the content of its faith manifested, this privileged soul not only believes but sees and experiences that the world is full of the glory of God.

The prophet Isaiah foresaw that in the latter days, the days of the Messiah, the earth would be full of the knowledge of the Lord as the waters cover the sea.[63] To the purified soul, the whole universe appears to be a great sea of love. "It seems to it that the entire universe is a sea of love in which it is engulfed, for, conscious of the living point or centre of love within itself, it is unable to catch sight of the boundaries of this love."[64] In the same way, the bride of the *Spiritual Canticle* is confronted with an unlimited horizon of beauty. And so, she is eager to go forth "To the mountain and to the hill, / To where the pure water flows".[65] The mountain is the beauty of divine wisdom, which is the Word of God. The hill is "the beauty of this other lesser wisdom, contained in His creatures and other mysterious works. This wisdom is also the beauty of the Son of God by which the soul desires to be illumined".[66]

The bride's song in these final stanzas is focused on the beauty of Jesus Christ, Son of God, and on the transformation he will work in her when she is united with him in heaven. "The Spouse will really transform her into the beauty of both His created and uncreated wisdom, and also into the beauty of the union of the Word with His humanity in which she will see Him face to face."[67]

NOTES

1 Brian McNeill *Christ in the Psalms*, Dublin, Veritas, 1988, p. 58

2 "Origenes cum in caeteris libris omnes vicerit, in Cantico canticorum ipse se vicit" quoted by Johannes Quasten in *Patrology*, Maryland, Christian Classics, 1983, vol. II, p. 50

3 Rabbi Aqiba, who died in AD 135, replied to another Jewish leader who said that the Song of Songs was not part of Scripture: "All the ages

are not worth the day on which the Song of Songs was given to Israel.
For all the writings are holy, but the Song of Songs is the holy of holies".
Brian McNeill *Christ in the Psalms*, p. 88

4   Johannes Quasten *Patrology*, vol II, p. 174
5   J.N.D. Kelly *Early Christian Doctrines*, London, Adam and Charles
Black, 1968, fourth edition, p. 78
6   Hosea 2; Isaiah 54: 4; Jeremiah 2: 2; Ezechiel 16 and 23
7   St Bernard in Cant., 52/2 quoted by Cuthbert Butler in *Western
Mysticism*, London, Constable, 1967, third edition p. 111
8   II *A.*, 20/6, *K.*, p. 378
9   Blaise Arminjon SJ *Cantata of Love*, Ignatius Press, 1988, p. 136
10 Henri de Lubac *Catholicism*, London, Burns and Oates, 1962, p. 193
11 *Sp.Cant.*, Prol. 1, *K.*, p. 408
12 *Sp.Cant.*, Prol. 1 and 2, *K.*, p. 408 and 409
13 *Sp.Cant.*, Prol. 2, *K.*, p. 409
14 *Sp.Cant.*, Prol. 3, *K.*, p. 409
15 *Sp.Cant.*, 13/9, *K.*, p. 460
16 *Sp.Cant.*, Stanza 1/2, *K.*, p. 416
17 *Sp.Cant.*, st. 1/20, *K.*, p. 423
18 *Sp.Cant.*, st. 1/5, *K.*, p. 417
19 *Sp.Cant.*, st. 1/11, *K.*, p. 420
20 *Sp.Cant.*, st. 1/11, *K.*, p. 420
21 St Thomas *Summa Theologica* translated by Fathers of the English
Dominican Province, Maryland, Christian Classics, I q 8 a 3, vol. I,
p. 36
22 *Sp.Cant.*, st. 11/3, *K.*, p. 449
23 *Sp.Cant.*, st. 11/4, *K.*, p. 449
24 *Sp.Cant.*, st. 1/6 and 7, *K.*, p. 418
25 *Sp.Cant.*, st. 1/9, *K.*, p. 419
26 II *D.N.*, 17/6, *K.*, p. 370
27 *L.F.*, III/28–67, *K.*, p. 620–37
28 *L.F.*, III/63 and 64, *K.*, p. 634 and 635
29 *Sp.Cant.*, st. 36/1, *K.*, p. 545
30 *Sp.Cant.*, st. 35/7, *K.*, p. 545
31 I *A.*, 2/5, *K.*, p. 75
32 *Sp.Cant.*, st. 11/4, *K.*, p. 449
33 *Sp.Cant.*, st. 1/22, *K.*, p. 424

34 *Sp.Cant.*, st. 13/1, *K.*, p. 457

35 *Sp.Cant.*, st. 9/5, *K.*, p. 444

36 *Sp.Cant.*, st. 9/6, *K.*, p. 444; st. 10/1, *K.*, p. 445

37 *Sp.Cant.*, st. 11/1, *K.*, p. 448

38 *Sp.Cant.*, st. 13/10, *K.*, p. 461

39 *Sp.Cant.*, st. 17/1, *K.*, p. 479

40 *Sp.Cant.*, st. 13/2, *K.*, p. 458

41 *Sp.Cant.*, st. 13/2, *K.*, p. 458

42 *Sp.Cant.*, st. 11/7, *K.*, p. 450

43 *Sp.Cant.*, st. 17/5, *K.*, p. 480

44 *Sp.Cant.*, st. 22/1, *K.*, p. 496

45 *Sp.Cant.*, st. 22/3, *K.*, p. 497

46 *Dialogue: Treatise on Prayer*, ch. 96

47 *Sp.Cant.*, st. 27/6, *K.*, p. 519

48 *Sp.Cant.*, st. 22/3, *K.*, p. 497

49 *Sp.Cant.*, st. 23/1, *K.*, p. 499

50 *Sp.Cant.*, st. 28/1, *K.*, p. 520; st. 32/1, *K.*, p. 534

51 *Sp.Cant.*, st. 28/4, *K.*, p. 521

52 *Sp.Cant.*, st. 27/8, *K.*, p. 519

53 *Sp.Cant.*, st. 33/3, *K.*, p. 538

54 *Sp.Cant.*, st. 33/7, *K.*, p. 539

55 *Sp.Cant.*, st. 34/1, *K.*, p. 540

56 *Sp.Cant.*, st. 34/2, *K.*, p. 541

57 *Sp.Cant.*, st. 39/8, 10, *K.*, p. 560

58 Crisogono de Jesus *The Life of St John of the Cross*, London, Long-mans, Green and Co., 1958, p. 134

59 St Thomas, Op. cit., II II q 180 a 2 ad 3

60 *Sp.Cant.*, st. 36/5, *K.*, p. 547

61 St Thomas, Op. cit., II II q 145 a 2 (St Thomas quoting Dionysius)

62 *Sp.Cant.*, st. 39/11, *K.*, p. 561

63 Isaiah 11: 9

64 *L.F.* st. 2/10, *K.*, p. 599

65 *Sp.Cant.*, stanza 36

66 *Sp.Cant.*, st. 36/7, *K.*, p. 548

67 *Sp.Cant.*, st. 38/1, *K.*, p. 553

15

THE LIVING FLAME
OF LOVE

St John of the Cross was in Granada between the years 1582 and 1585. A devout widow called Ana de Penelosa had loaned her house to the Carmelite nuns when they were making a foundation in that city. St John wrote some verses for her (four six-line stanzas), beginning with the words, "O living flame of love". The title was: "Stanzas which the soul recites in the intimate union with God, its beloved Bridegroom". Dona Ana then asked for some explanation of the poem. He felt reluctant to give an explanation, he said, because the stanzas deal with matters so interior and spiritual, for which words are usually lacking. Another reason he gave was that one speaks badly of the intimate depths of the spirit if one does not do so with a deeply recollected soul. He deferred writing until a period "in which the Lord seems to have uncovered some knowledge and bestowed some fervour". He was encouraged to write by the thought that his reader "understands that everything I say is as far from the reality as is a painting from the living object represented".[1] In what he wrote, St John's own soul is revealed. "The *Living Flame of Love* is a book of fire. Written all at a stretch in a fortnight, under the influence of an intense love, it reveals the Saint's ardent soul better than the other works."[2]

The *Living Flame* and the *Spiritual Canticle* deal with the same high degree of perfect union with God, the spiritual marriage, total transformation in the Beloved. The *Living Flame* focuses on

179

certain acts of love within that state, acts of a deeper quality and rare perfection. Love can always receive added quality and become more intense. We might say that, whereas the *Canticle* moves forward horizontally from simple union to betrothal, to mystical marriage, the *Flame* has only a vertical movement. The imagery of fire and flame bring out this difference. The soul is so inwardly transformed in the fire of love and has received such quality from it that it is not only united to this fire but the fire becomes within it a living flame. St John had already used the figure of the log of wood put into a furnace. The wood first becomes black and ugly; it is drained dry of its tears and becomes shrivelled. As the fire grows hotter and continues to burn "the wood becomes much more incandescent and inflamed, even to the point of flaring up and shooting out flames from itself".[3] It is of this degree of enkindled love that the soul speaks in the *Living Flame*. It suffers no longer. The flame no longer afflicts or distresses, as it did in the beginning when the flame was not so friendly and gentle towards it as it is now in this state of union. The soul addresses the flame therefore in words of intimate delicacy and love: "O living flame of love / That tenderly wounds my soul in its deepest centre."

> This flame of love is the Spirit of its Bridegroom, which is the Holy Spirit. The soul feels Him within itself not only as a fire which has consumed and transformed it, but as a fire that burns and flares within it, as I mentioned. And that flame, every time it flares up, bathes the soul in glory and refreshes it with the quality of divine life. Such is the activity of the Holy Spirit in the soul transformed in love: the interior acts He produces shoot up flames for they are acts of inflamed love, in which the will of the soul united with that flame, made one with it, loves most sublimely.[4]

These acts of inflamed love are one with the action of the Holy

Spirit, and take the soul to the peak of its upward striving. One act of this kind is more precious and of more value to the Church and the world than all other works a person may have done during a whole lifetime. In the commentary, St John maintains a very exalted level of thought as he describes this profound theological reality. The whole Trinity is at work in the soul, each divine Person bestowing a gift that produces a distinct effect. The delightful wound of love is attributed to the Holy Spirit, the taste of eternal life to the delicate touch of the Son, the transformation of the soul to the gentle hand of the Father. "The soul now feels that it is all inflamed in the divine union, and that its palate is all bathed in glory and love, that in the most intimate part of its substance it is flooded with no less than rivers of glory . . . "[5] Every time the delicate flame of love assails the soul, it does so as though glorifying it with gentle and powerful glory.

The direct vision of God is not possible in this life, where we must remains always within the order of faith. For beatific vision, the soul needs the gift of a new power, the light of glory. What the soul does in heaven by means of that powerful light, it does on earth after its own fashion, by means of a highly illumined faith, but on a plane notably lower than the beatific vision. Contemplative lights perfect the supernatural life on earth, but they cannot bring it to the perfection of the next life. The impassible gulf between the two realms is expressed in the *Spiritual Canticle* as a painful experience of souls after they have gone out in search of the Beloved: "For an immense good is shown them, as through the fissure of a rock, but not granted them. Thus their pain and torment is unspeakable".[6] In the *Living Flame*, however, the soul perceives much more clearly the power of the next life and the fragility of the present one. It feels that the veil between them is of very delicate texture, as thin as a spider's web, so "very spiritual, thin and luminous, that it does not prevent the divinity from vaguely appearing through it".[7] As might be expected, the soul addresses the *Living Flame* with a petition, "if it be Your will", to "tear through" the veil abruptly, without even the delay of cutting or destroying.

St John admits that we are dealing here with very rare experiences. He knows that some people will either fail to believe them or consider the account of them an exaggeration.

> Yet I reply to all these persons that the Father of lights (James 1:17), who is not closefisted but diffuses Himself abundantly, as the sun does its rays, without being a respector of persons (Acts 10:34), wherever there is room – always showing Himself gladly along the highways and byways – does not hesitate or consider it of little import to find His delights with the children of men at a common table in the world. (Proverbs 8:31)[8]

Even before beginning his commentary on the *Flame*, St John knew that the sublime graces he was about to describe would not seem credible to many readers. In a paragraph of the Prologue, he dispels any doubts we might have:

> There is no reason to marvel at God's granting such sublime and strange gifts to souls He determines to favour. If we consider that He is God and that He bestows them as God, with infinite love and goodness, it does not seem unreasonable. For He declared that the Father, the Son, and the Holy Spirit would take up their abode in anyone who loved Him. (John 14:23) He takes up His abode in a man by making him live the life of God and dwell in the Father, the Son, and the Holy Spirit, as the soul points out in these stanzas.[9]

THE GLORY OF THE LORD

The "glory of the Lord" was used in the Bible to denote the presence of God as it materialized on the mountain or in the temple, in the form of fire or smoke. "Now the appearance of the glory of the Lord was like a devouring fire on the top of the mountain in the sight of the people of Israel."[10] The Greek word *doxa* (glory) became the term for the manner in which the majesty of God was outwardly manifested, revealed and concealed. This traditional "glory of the Lord", the radiant fire of his presence, became in New Testament times the "glory" of Christ. The word *doxa* was purposely used in the gospels to suggest the divinity of Christ. Jesus manifested his glory in certain acts of power, like the changing of water into wine. Glory was to be revealed most of all in *the* great acts of divine power, the death and resurrection of Jesus. That was why, in his priestly prayer, the offertory prayer of his sacrifice, Jesus prayed: "Father, glorify your Son that your Son may glorify You." The answer to this prayer could not take place until his "hour" had come. And so, in St John's gospel, the meaning of "glory" changes gradually until the final "hour" when it no longer signifies outward manifestation but the inward action of sacrificial love. As one commentator puts it: " ... the glorification of Jesus, begun by signs, culminates in a death accepted in love, as the very act by which the Father glorifies him and he the Father".[11] Because Jesus was God as well as man, the moment of his death was a supreme moment in history. His "hour" changed the whole character of our existence. An eternal liturgy of praise now rises up from the earth. All honour and glory is given to the Father by his Son in the unity of their common Spirit, who has now been given to us.

The *Living Flame of Love* is located in this doxology. The "flame" is the same Holy Spirit, whose activity has transformed the soul so that it can now love "most sublimely". Christ's priestly prayer is verified: "The glory which thou hast given me I have given to them" (John 17:22). God glorifies the soul that the soul may glorify Him. After having been buried in the "sepulchre of dark death", the soul is now absorbed in the intimate life of

God, "its palate all bathed in glory and love". This foretaste of glory does not consist of a blaze of light that could be perceived in a material way. Essentially, it is a participation in the acts by which God knows and loves himself. Because of the supreme delight and joy that God finds in his own excellence, he has willed that others outside of himself should participate in this supreme good. This becomes a pinnacle of human activity when the soul is privileged with an intimate sharing in the innumerable attributes of God. For these then become in the soul real "lamps of fire", both illumination and warmth of love, giving back to God a perfect praise.

> O Lamps of fire!
> In whose splendours
> The deep caverns of feeling,
> Once obscure and blind,
> Now give forth, so rarely, so exquisitely,
> Both warmth and light to their Beloved.[12]

The habitual state of the soul is one of transformation in God, but its activity does not always reach the exalted level of being illumined "within the splendours of God". Nevertheless, sometimes the burning log is seen to flare up so that it becomes one with the flame of the Holy Spirit.

The movements of these divine flames, which are the flickering and flaring up we have mentioned, are not alone produced by the soul that is transformed in the flames of the Holy Spirit, nor does the Holy Spirit produce them alone, but they are the work of both the soul and Him, since He moves it in the manner that fire moves the enkindled air. Thus these movements of both God and the soul are not only splendours, but also glorifications of the soul . . . It seems in these that He is always wanting to bestow eternal life and transport it completely to perfect glory by bringing it into Himself.[13]

In this state of perfect union, a reciprocal love is formed between God and the soul, "like the marriage union and surrender". St John notes the refinement with which the soul makes this surrender. Its bearing before God is of rare excellence in regard to its love, and its gratitude, and its praise. Firstly, it loves God now not through itself but through God. It loves through the Holy Spirit, as the Father and the Son love each other. Secondly, it loves God in God, "for in this union the soul is vehemently absorbed in love of God, and God in great vehemence surrenders Himself to the soul".[14] Thirdly, it loves Him on account of who he is, not because of what it receives from him. This is "pure delight" to the soul without any admixture of its own pleasure. Because God has now surrenderd himself to the soul, the fundamental longing of the soul is realized: it can give to God as great a love as it receives.

> It is conscious there that God is indeed its own and that it possesses Him by inheritance, with the right of ownership, as His adopted son, through the grace of His gift of Himself. Having Him for its own, it can give Him and communicate Him to whomever it wishes. Thus it gives Him to its Beloved, who is the very God who gave Himself to it. By this donation it repays God for all it owes Him, since it willingly gives as much as it receives from Him.[15]

St John did not want to speak much of this wonderful transforming work of the Holy Spirit, "filled for the soul with good and glory and delicate love of God, for I am aware of being incapable of so doing, and were I to try, it might seem less than it is".[16]

The soul is filled not only with "delicate love" but also with a corresponding knowledge; the living flame gives out both warmth and light (stanza 3). The light of the flame awakens the soul "from the sleep of natural vision to supernatural vision". This is not the beatific vision but a knowledge and experience of

God that is "entirely beyond words". The excellences it perceives in God awaken the soul; "an immense, powerful voice sounds in it, the voice of a multitude of excellences, of thousands of virtues in God, infinite in number". At the end of the Song of Songs there is a similar awakening, which has been interpreted as "a rebirth to a new life . . . the very word of the Resurrection".[17] St John's account of it authenticates him as a true teacher of divine wisdom and gives us an insight into the wonder of God's communion with those who respond to his love:

> How gently and lovingly
> You wake in my heart,

There are many kinds of awakening which God effects in the soul, so many that we would never finish explaining them all. Yet this awakening of the Son of God, which the soul refers to here, is one of the most elevated and most beneficial. For this awakening is a movement of the Word in the substance of the soul, containing such grandeur, dominion, and glory, and intimate sweetness that it seems to the soul that all the balsams and fragrant spices and flowers of the world are commingled, stirred, and shaken so as to yield their sweet odour, and that all the kingdoms and dominions of the world and all the powers and virtues of heaven are moved; and not only this, but it also seems that all the virtues and substances and perfections and graces of every created thing glow and make the same movement all at once . . .

Even this comparison is most inadequate, for in this awakening they not only seem to move, but they all likewise disclose the beauties of their being, power, loveliness, and graces, and the root of their duration and life. For the soul is conscious of how all creatures, earthly and heavenly, have their life, duration, and strength in Him . . .[18]

SUMMARY

The *Living Flame of Love* deals with a very exalted level of spiritual activity, which many readers may find somewhat overwhelming. The state of divine love which it describes is not amenable to analysis. Nevertheless, the book as a whole may become easier to read if we distinguish four different areas of activity corresponding to the four stanzas of the poem.

Stanza 1. *The Holy Spirit* – The stanza is addressed to the Holy Spirit, who is both power and tenderness to a supreme degree. His activity in the soul was formerly experienced as oppressive. Now it is all tenderness, because the soul is no longer in opposition to it. The plea now is that the Holy Spirit would complete his work, break the last thread, and take the soul into eternal life.

Stanza 2. *The Blessed Trinity* – The soul experiences the presence of the three Persons of the Trinity, distinguishing them by the special effect each of them produces. The *gentle hand* is the merciful and omnipotent Father. The *delicate touch* is the Word, the Son of God. The *delightful wound, the sweet cautery*, is the Holy Spirit.

Stanza 3. *The One God* – The experience of the indwelling of the Blessed Trinity is also an experience of the soul's own infinite capacity. Formerly, the soul was not conscious of its "deep caverns" because it was not so utterly emptied. Now it experiences an infinite thirst for God, who is perceived as an aggregate of innumerable perfections. Each of these perfections is God, and all of them are one perfection. They are now lamps of fire, filling the "deep caverns" of the soul, giving back "both warmth and light to their Beloved", delighting God with reflectons of his own splendour.

Stanza 4. *Divine Life* – The Bridegroom awakens in the perfect soul, and gives it a foretaste of the light of the Resurrection.

"And in that awakening, which is as though one were to awaken and breathe, the soul feels a strange delight in the breathing of the Holy Spirit in God, in which it is sovereignly glorified and taken with love."

NOTES

1   *L.F.*, Prol. 1, *K.*, p. 577
2   Fr Gabriel of St Mary Magdalen ODC, *St John of the Cross*, translated by a Benedictine of Stanbrook Abbey, Cork, Mercier Press, 1946, p. 81
3   *L.F.*, Prol. 3, *K.*, p. 578
4   *L.F.*, 1/3, *K.*, p. 580
5   *L.F.*, 1/1, *K.*, p. 579
6   *Sp.Cant.*, 1/22, *K.*, p. 424
7   *L.F.*, 1/32, *K.*, p. 592
8   *L.F.*, 1/15, *K.*, p. 584–5
9   *L.F.*, Prol. 2, *K.*, p. 577
10 Exodus 24:17 (RSV)
11 Dom Ralph Russell *A New Catholic Commentary on Holy Scripture*; St John, p. 1034 (no. 798 f). General Editor, Rev. Reginald C. Fuller DD, Thomas Nelson and Sons, Ltd, London, 1969
    For the word *doxa* see Geoffrey W. Bromily, *Theological Dictionary of the New Testament*, p. 178–81, William B. Eerdmans Publishing Company, The Paternoster Press, Exeter, Devon
12 *L.F.*, stanza 3, *K.*, p. 610
13 *L.F.*, 3/10, *K.*, p. 614–15
14 *L.F.*, 3/82, *K.*, p. 642
15 *L.F.*, 3/78, *K.*, p. 641
16 *L.F.*, 4/17, *K.*, p. 649
17 Blaise Arminjon SJ *The Cantata of Love*, Ignatius Press, 1988, p. 342
18 *L.F.*, 4/4, 5, *K.*, p. 644

APPENDIX

ST JOHN'S
THREE SIGNS OF
CONTEMPLATION

[*Author's note*: This excellent piece of research was done by Dr Liz Carmichael. It is a valuable contribution to the understanding of the three signs in St John's writings.]

In the *Ascent of Mount Carmel* (II.13), and again in the *Dark Night* (I.9), St John of the Cross gives three signs by which the "night of sense" may be recognized. They mark the transition from active meditation to the prayer of loving attention which is the beginning of contemplation.

One has only to consider the methods of imaginative meditation that are again popular in our own time through the Ignatian revival, or read, if one has the opportunity, the sixteenth century works of Luis de Granada on prayer and meditation, with their very full and beautiful considerations of the meaning of the Gospel, to understand the active forms of prayer of which St John was speaking. He stands in a tradition that was already firmly established when he teaches that these forms are a training and education of the mind, heart, and will, which then enable the person to pass safely into the simpler prayer of contemplation. For his three signs, he had a specific source in a work attributed in his time to the German Dominican preacher John Tauler (*c.* 1300–61).

Tauler's work had considerable authority because of his reputation as a good and holy pastor. His own teaching is to be found in his sermons, and he does indeed speak of the night of sense and of passing into contemplation; but when the Carthusian scholar Laurence Surius collected all the writings ascribed to him and printed a Latin translation of them in Cologne in 1548, he included another work, which he said had recently been "discovered", an *Institutions* (or "instructions"), which he assumed to be Tauler's. There is a short passage on the *Institutions* in the book by a Stanbrook Benedictine, *Mediaeval Mystical Tradition and St John of the Cross* (1954, p. 101–4). The author does not tell us the source of her information, but states that the *Institutions* is a compendium of excerpts from various German writers of Tauler's time: two of the 39 chapters (there are 39 in all the versions, not 38 as the Benedictine suggests) are in fact from his sermons; and some others are passages from Ruysbroeck and Eckhart.

Sometimes under the title *Institutions*, or sometimes as the *Medulla Animae* ("centre of the soul"), this work took on a popularity of its own and was published in Castilian in 1551, Dutch 1557, French 1587, Italian 1590, and High German 1681. With the exception of the Dutch and probably the German, which were done from the Oberland dialect original (which does not itself seem to have been printed: at least, if it was, there is no copy in the Bodleian or British libraries), these translations all seem to have been made from Surius's Latin version. There was no translation into English.

During his time as a student at Salamanca, if not before, John must almost certainly have had access to the Latin translation. He is said to have written a short thesis on contemplation, for which the *Institutions* would have been a useful resource. But it is also quite likely that he first knew this work in Castilian. According to our Benedictine informant, this Spanish translation was first printed in Coimbra in 1551; but the copy in the British Library is a reprint done in Medina del Campo in 1554, when John was living there aged twelve. It was on sale at the shop of Guillermo de Millis "behind the main church" in Medina. A poor boy could not have bought it, but perhaps John somehow came to know it over the next few years – possibly even before he became a Carmelite.

THE THREE SIGNS IN THE *INSTITUTIONS*

The chapter in which the three signs are discussed is Chapter 35. Its author has not been identified, and although its teaching is like that of Tauler's its style strongly suggests it is from another hand. The chapter begins by emphasizing that imaginative and discursive meditation are good and necessary. They help us to be converted from sin, and are the means by which we come to know the life and teaching of our Lord. Nevertheless there comes a time when it is right to set these means aside, and pass into a more imageless and passive way of prayer – and there are three signs that show when this moment has come:

> Caeterum tria sunt, ex quibus adverti potest, quando iam dictae imagines abdicandae sint, ne vel citius quam oportet repudientur, vel nimis diu eisdem inhaereatur. Primum est, quando quicquid unquam auditu percepimus vel intellectu, cum taedio respicimus. Secundum, quando quicquid audimus vel intelligimus, nulla nos delectatione afficit. Tertium, cum intra nos esuriem desideriumque summi boni illius, quod tamen appraehendere non valemus, magis ac magis crescere sentimus, ita ut dicamus: Domine Deus meus, ultra iam procedere nequeo. Orare meum est, annuere tuum. Haec tria quisquis in seipso depraehenderit, non solum poterit, sed et debebit eas, de quibus praedixerimus, imagines sanctas, et opera rationabiliter abdicare.[1]

This can be translated:

> To continue, there are three things by which it can be known
> when the aforesaid images are to be abandoned, so that they
> neither be set aside sooner than is fitting, nor clung to for too
> long a time. The first is when we regard with weary distaste
> anything that we have at any time received with the hearing or
> the intellect. The second, when whatever we hear or under-
> stand affects us with no feeling of delight. The third, when we
> feel growing more and more within us a hunger and longing
> for that highest good, which nevertheless we have not the
> strength to grasp, so much so that we say: My Lord God, I am
> not able to proceed further. It is mine to pray, yours to reward.
> Whoever has detected these three within himself, will not only
> be able with good reason, to set aside those holy imaginings
> and active thinking of which we have spoken, but he also
> should do so.

I have translated *imagines* as "imaginings" because what is being
referred to is the imaginative method of meditation, and *opera* as
"active thinking" because that is the kind of "work" that is
meant. In the Castilian the terms are "*imaginaciones y considerationes*". The Spanish translator adopted a conversational style
and the whole passage in Castilian reads as follows:

> Pero os de advertir quando se han de posponer las dichas
> imaginaciones, porque no se dexen mas temprano ni se
> retengan por mas tiempo que conviene. Para lo qual pongo
> tres señales. La primera quando ya el hombre viene a tal
> estado que oyendo, o entendiendo algo dellas recibe hastio.
> La segunda quando oyendo o tratando dellas ningun deleyte
> recibe. La tercera quando sentimos crescer en nosotros la
> hambre y desseo de aquel summo bien que aun no podemos
> alcançar, tanto que digamos: Señor Dios mio ya no puedo

passar adelante. Mio es pedirte, de ti solo es conceder lo que pido. Quien estas tres cosas en si experimentare, no solamente podra, mas convenirle ha dexar las sanctas imaginaciones, y considerationes que diximos.[2]

But I must advise you as to when the aforementioned imaginative meditations should be left behind, so that they neither be left earlier nor retained for a longer time than is necessary. For which, I give three signs. The first, when a person reaches such a state that on hearing or understanding anything of these things, he receives weariness. The second, when listening to or dealing with them he receives no pleasure. The third, when we feel growing in ourselves the hunger and desire for that highest good which we still cannot reach, so much so that we say: My Lord God, I cannot proceed further. It is mine to ask, and yours alone to give what I ask. Whoever experiences these three things in himself not only would be able, but ought, to leave behind the holy imagining and active thinking of which we have spoken.

There is only one significant difference between the Latin and the Castilian. Where Surius had the perfect tense, *percepimus*, the Spanish translator has the present, so that he says: "The first, when . . . on hearing or understanding anything of these things [imaginative meditations], he receives weariness" – and here St John tends to follow the Castilian, concentrating on the present situation in prayer rather than on the feeling that all that has ever been experienced in the world of sense has turned to dust. It seems likely that the original author had the past tense, because the Dutch translation is also in the past: "*alle dat ghi oyt hoorde oft verstont*", "all that you have ever heard or understood" (1557 edition, p. 195, unnumbered).

ST JOHN'S THREE SIGNS

At *Ascent* II.13, 1–5, John closely echoes the teaching of Chapter 35. He writes: "discursive meditation (a work through images, forms, and figures)" is good and necessary because "by these sensitive means beginners dispose their spirit and habituate it to spiritual things, and at the same time they void their senses of all other base, temporal, secular, and natural forms and images"; but at the proper time, neither too soon nor after an unnecessary delay, it will be right to abandon these practices (13.1). The three signs John provides here are that the person: (i) ceases to receive the satisfaction that they formerly derived from discursive meditation (13.2); (ii) becomes disinclined to fix the imagination and sense faculties on any particular object, interior or exterior (13.3); (iii) is content to remain in a general loving awareness of God, "without any particular knowledge or understanding" (13.4).

St John outlines three signs again at *Dark Night* I.9: (i) no pleasure is received from anything, earthly or heavenly (9.2); (ii) the remembrance of God is present, and there is a deep care for the things of God despite the painful lack of delight in them (9.3–7); (iii) there is an inability to meditate discursively and make use of the imagination as one had done before (9.8).

Perhaps there are essentially two aspects of this state: there is dryness because the world of sense is no longer enough, and there is a deep longing for God himself and for Him to lead us beyond where we have any capacity for going ourselves. The various sets of signs are different ways of describing the experience of a person who comes to this point.

The original author (who liked to set things out in threes) created a trio by inverting the first sign (tedium) to make a second (lack of delight), so his first and second signs are the positive and negative aspects of dryness. St John makes dryness a single sign, marked equally by distaste and lack of delight (*Ascent* (i) = *Dark Night* (i)). Meanwhile the third sign in the *Institutions* comprehended both human helplessness, and the soul's longing for God. St John separates these two components, distinguishing between the impossibility of proceeding by one's own efforts on the one hand (*A.* (ii) = *DN* (iii)), and the longing to serve God, or contentedness to rest in God, on the other (*A* (iii) = *DN* (ii)). So while both the author of Chapter 35 and St John of the Cross have three signs, and while the substance of their teaching is the same, they divide the substance differently between the signs. Perhaps the ideal would be to conflate them, and have four signs!

Finally, what of the significance of these signs today? They still have all their force; and they can be present in people who have not spent years in discursive meditation. The educative work of conversion and the formation of the intellect and will, that was normally accomplished by formal meditation in John's day (and may still be so accomplished today), is now likely to have been done by a variety of other means: group Bible study, reading, sermons, retreats, even TV. St John has no doubt of the profound necessity for such formation. Alongside it, many find that they are attracted to a simple prayer of loving attention, like that of Taizé, from quite early on. St John still points us further, beyond all human means and through the crises of darkness and detachment that must occur, to the riches and depths and heights of contemplative prayer.

Dr Liz Carmichael, Worcester College, Oxford, 1990

NOTES

Johannis Tauleri, *Opera Omnia*, edited and translated from the German by Laurence Surius, Cologne 1548: folio 2, p. lxviii. Bodleian

RECOMMENDED READING

Blaise Arminjon *The Cantata of Love: A Verse-by-Verse Reading of the Song of Songs*, translated by Nelly Marans. San Francisco, Ignatius Press, 1989.

Hans Urs von Balthasar *The Glory of the Lord*, Edinburgh, T. & T. Clark. Volume III contains a seventy-page study of St John of the Cross.

Gerald Brenan *St John of the Cross: His Life and Poetry*, with a translation of the poetry by Lynda Nicholson. Cambridge University Press, 1973.

Fr Bruno OCD *St John of the Cross*, with an introduction by Jacques Maritain. London, Sheed & Ward, 1936.

Fr Crisogono de Jesus *The Life of St John of the Cross*, translated by Kathleen Pond. London, Longmans, Green & Co. Ltd, 1958.

Alain Cugno *St John of the Cross: The Life and Thought of a Christian Mystic*, translated by Barbara Wale. London, Burns & Oates, 1982.

E.W. Truman Dicken *The Crucible of Love*, a study of the mystical doctrine of St Teresa and St John of the Cross. London, 1963.

Thomas Dubay SM *Fire Within: St Teresa of Avila, St John of the Cross, and the Gospel – on Prayer*. San Francisco, Ignatius Press, 1989.

Richard P. Hardy *The Life of St John of the Cross: Search for Nothing*. London, Darton, Longman & Todd, 1982.

Fr Gregory D'Souza OCD *Transforming Flame: Spiritual Anthropology of St John of the Cross*. India, Divya Jyothi Publications, 1988.

Thomas Green SJ *When the Well Runs Dry: Prayer beyond the Beginnings*. Indiana, Notre Dame, 1979.

Fr John Venard OCD *The Spiritual Canticle of St John of the Cross*, simplified version with notes. Australia, E.J. Dwyer, 1980.

George H. Tavard *Poetry and Contemplation in St John of the Cross*. Ohio University Press, 1988.

E. Allison Peers *Spirit of Flame*. London, 1963, reprinted 1978.

Edith Stein *The Science of the Cross*, translated by Hilda Graef. London, 1960.

Rowan Williams *The Wound of Knowledge: Christian Spirituality from the New Testament to St John of the Cross*. London, Darton, Longman & Todd, revised edition, 1990.

D. Tillyer *Union with God: The Teaching of St John of the Cross*. London, 1984.

On the question of the two redactions of the *Spiritual Canticle*:

E. Allison Peers *The Complete Works of St John of the Cross*, Vol. II. London, Burns, Oates and Washbourne Ltd, 1934. Introduction, pp. 8–22.

Edith Stein *The Science of the Cross: A Study of St John of the Cross*, translated by Hilda Graef. London, Burns and Oates, 1960, pp. 175–183.